Faith and Reason

Faith and Reason:

An Introduction to Modern Jewish Thought

SAMUEL HUGO BERGMAN

Translated and Edited

by ALFRED JOSPE

A Hillel Book

SCHOCKEN BOOKS · NEW YORK

This volume is one of a series of "Hillel Little Books." Developed by the B'nai B'rith Hillel Foundations, the books in this series deal with issues of fundamental importance to Jewish college students. Written by men of variant points of view, they are intended to stimulate further study and discussion.

First SCHOCKEN PAPERBACK *edition 1963*

Third Printing, 1968

This edition is published by arrangement with B'nai B'rith Hillel Foundations, Inc.

Library of Congress Catalog Card No. 61-10414

Manufactured in the United States of America

CONTENTS

Faith and Reason

FOREWORD

The manuscript of this book grew out of a series of lectures which Dr. Samuel Hugo Bergman delivered in Europe several years ago. The selection of the personalities who were included in the series was influenced by autobiographical considerations: the author wanted to deal primarily with those thinkers who had been his "teachers" — who had influenced the development of his Jewish thinking decisively or enriched his understanding of the problems of faith and reason.

For this reason, Dr. Bergman does not present a complete study of each thinker's total system but concentrates on an analysis of the two major issues which he considers of paramount importance for the Jew in our time: How does the thinker resolve the tension between faith and reason, and how does he answer the question whether there still is a distinctively or uniquely Jewish way to God? Dr. Bergman's analysis makes a significant contribution to an understanding of what faith itself means, and it is published by the B'nai B'rith Hillel Foundations as a resource for reading, study and discussion among thoughtful "students" of all ages because we share Dr. Bergman's conviction that "men who have spoken in and to our age can probably give us a deeper insight . . . . than men of earlier centuries into the nature and meaning of faith" and its relevance for the modern Jew.

The translation is based on the original German text of the lectures as well as on several chapters of Dr. Bergman's recent volume, *Hogim u-maaminim*, Jerusalem 1959. An earlier translation of the German lectures by Dr. Emil Fackenheim, Associate Professor of Philosophy, University of Toronto, was very helpful to me but used sparingly because the original text, on which his translation had been based, was thoroughly revised for this Hillel edition. I wish to record my gratitude and indebtedness to Dr. Fackenheim for his generous counsel; to Dr. Lou Silberman, Hillel Professor of Jewish Thought and Literature at Vanderbilt University, for his editorial assistance on the chapter on Martin Buber; to Dr. Maurice Friedman, of Sarah Lawrence College, for his clarification of certain aspects of Buber's thought; and to Dr. Maurice Zigmond, Hillel's New England Regional Director, for his technical assistance in the preparation of the manuscript.

The quotations from Nahum N. Glatzer, *Franz Rosenzweig*, are used by permission of Schocken Books, Inc.; the quotation from J. L. Magnes, *In the Perplexity of the Times*, is used by permission of the Magnes Press of the Hebrew University.

A. J.

Chapter One

FAITH AND REASON

This book deals with men of faith in our time. However, it wants to do more than tell the story of their lives. Their ideas and experiences may help us discover what faith itself means. Men who have spoken in and to our own age can probably give us a deeper insight into the nature and meaning of faith than men of earlier centuries; and after we have listened to the language of faith in our time we may be in a better position to understand the classical documents of faith as well.

Modern man finds it difficult to understand what faith is; he finds it even more difficult to have faith. Faith requires the ability to *listen*. It is for this reason that the watch-word of Judaism opens with the word "shema" — "Hear." Modern man, however, rarely pauses to listen. He is rarely alone. He is "busy" — surrounded by crowds, engulfed by noise, submerged in his work or strenuously absorbed in leisure-time activities. He lacks the peace in which alone the still small voice of faith can speak.

Above all, many people face an intellectual difficulty as they attempt to explore the meaning of faith. The claims of faith seem to contradict the findings of reason and they feel they cannot accept the propositions of faith without surrendering their intellectual integrity.

The conflict between faith and reason has long been known, and it has been widely discussed since it emerged in the Middle Ages under the influence of Greek philosophy. The three monotheistic religions had defined faith as a special source of truth, as a well-spring of objective knowledge which complemented human reason yet was distinct from and independent of it. Faith and reason were conceived as separate sources of truth and knowledge. But this definition of faith posed more questions than it resolved. Can there be two sources of truth? Is reason, in principle, incapable of discovering the truth revealed by faith, or can this truth be demonstrated and verified by reason? Indeed, can anything be "true" unless it can be demonstrated and verified by reason? Each new answer posed new questions.

I

We can understand the true nature of faith, or at least of Biblical faith, only if we recognize the fundamental fact that any definition of faith which considers it a special source of truth is wrong in principle. Faith is not a special source of truth independent of reason or opposed to it. The Biblical term for faith, *emunah*, designates an attitude of trust and confidence between man and God. To have *emunah* is not to claim that a certain proposition is logically true. It is to "entrust" oneself to God and to feel secure in this trust. The believer, as Shalom Ben Chorin put it, "does not believe *in* God; he believes Him." Buber expresses the same thought when he writes that "Biblical man is never in doubt as to the existence of God. In professing his faith, his *emunah*, he merely expresses his trust that the living God is near to him as he was to Abraham and that he entrusts himself to Him."[1]

Such immediate certainty is not restricted to the realm of religious faith. Each of us is immediately certain of the existence of his fellowman. Every encounter with another person, every conversation or handshake assure me with immediate certainty that I am not alone in the world. It may be a legitimate philosophical problem to inquire whether I can prove the existence of anyone other than myself. Indeed, the history of philosophy knows of solipsists, thinkers who in all sincerity question or deny the existence of a "thou" on the assumption that the self is the only existent being and can know nothing but its own modifications and states. The problem may have philosophical interest and is probably not easily resolved. The point, however, is that whenever I take the hand of a friend and say "thou" to him, I do not relate myself to him on the level of philosophical argument and detached "objective" analysis; I enter into a relationship of immediate certainty, immediate trust, immediate faith.

Faith is a relationship which has an immediacy analogous to that which exists between an "I" and a "thou." The believer *encounters* God. He knows God's hand is extended to him. He speaks to God and receives an answer. He prays to Him, being just as certain of His existence as he is of his own or that of his neighbor. He requires no proof for this supreme certainty; yet should others desire proof he cannot provide it. He cannot offer objective evidence for what, in his heart, he knows to be utterly true and real.

The Biblical story of Samuel's call offers a graphic description of the nature and meaning of faith.

> "And the child Samuel ministered unto the Lord before Eli. And the word of the Lord was precious in those days; there was no frequent vision. And it came to pass in that time, when Eli was laid down in his place — now his eyes had begun to wax dim so that he could not see — and the lamp of God was not yet gone out, and Samuel was laid down to sleep in the temple of the Lord, where the ark of God was, that the Lord called Samuel; and he said: 'Here am I.' And he ran unto Eli and said: 'Here am I; for thou didst call me.' And he said: 'I called not; lie down again.' And he went and lay down. And the Lord called yet again Samuel. And Samuel arose and went to Eli and said: 'Here am I, for thou didst call me.' And he answered: 'I called not, my son; lie down again.' Now Samuel did not yet know the Lord, neither was the word of the Lord yet revealed unto him. And the Lord called Samuel again the third time. And he arose and went to Eli, and said: 'Here am I; for thou didst call me.' And Eli perceived that the Lord was calling the child. Therefore Eli said unto Samuel: 'Go, lie down; and it shall be, if thou be called, that thou shalt say: Speak, Lord; for Thy servant heareth.' "[2]

Samuel hears himself called by name in the darkness of the night. Eli did not hear the voice even though he and Samuel were sleeping in the same room. The experience was subjective, private. But Eli knew enough of the nature of revelation to realize that only one of those who were present might be chosen to receive it. Therefore he urged the boy to await a further call, although he himself had heard nothing. Had Eli doubted that a voice had spoken to Samuel, the boy could have done nothing to "prove" its reality. The faith in the "efficacious presence" (*présence efficace*), to use Henri Bergson's phrase, is not capable of objective proof and cannot be supported by objective evidence.

Gandhi defined faith as encounter in the same way when he spoke of the small voice within which had accompanied him through life and to which he had trained himself to listen through mental and physical exercises:

> "I have no way of convincing the skeptic of the existence of this voice. He is at liberty to say that it is a delusion or hallucination. It may be so. I cannot prove its existence. But what I can say is that the unanimous contradiction of the entire world will not weaken me in my faith that what I have heard is the voice of God. To me this voice is more real than my own existence."[3]

The act of faith is grounded in this immediacy of experience, in the certainty of the believer that it is God who spoke or speaks to him. However, the believer faces two difficulties. Others may demand proof, "objective" evidence for his claim that the experience was real and that the encounter took place. And he himself may come to doubt at a later moment whether the encounter had been real — for the grace of the hallowed moment does not last beyond its immediacy. The life of faith is intermittent. Moments of immediacy are rare, as Maimonides had already pointed out in the introduction to his *Guide of the Perplexed*:

> "At times, the truth shines so brilliantly that we perceive it as clear as day. Our nature and habit then draw a veil over our perception, and we return to a darkness almost as dense as before. We are like those who, though beholding frequent flashes of lightning, still find themselves in the thickest darkness of the night. On some, the lightning flashes in rapid succession, and they seem to be in continuous light, and their night is clear as the day. . . . By others only once during the whole night is a flash of lightning perceived. . . . And there are some to whom the flashes of lightning appear at varying intervals."[4]

Maimonides recognized that religious immediacy is intermittent. But the life of faith cannot rest solely on intermittent religious experiences. There must be something that will validate the truth of faith when they are absent, something less subjective and personal and hence more "objective" and rational that will bridge the gap between them.

It is at this point that reason and knowledge have a place in the realm of faith. Consider, for instance, the role which the Bible plays in religious life. The Bible itself cannot be a source of faith: the reading of the Biblical text cannot be a substitute for that immediate experience in which the act of faith is grounded. But the Bible speaks of the faith of others. It describes their encounter with God and confronts us with the heritage of faith of the centuries. We probably cannot understand the Bible fully unless we ourselves had some kind of religious experience, no matter how weak or inadequate. Then, however, the Bible can strengthen our faith by exposing us to the example of others; the record of their struggles and experiences, the example of their discoveries and defeats can deepen our understanding of the nature and meaning of faith. The knowledge of what faith has meant and means to others can clarify and fortify our own faith.

This knowledge is, of course, not the kind of knowledge which "proves" that the claims of faith are true. It is knowledge of other people's faith — of the fact that they had a faith similar to or identical with that to which we ourselves may aspire. Knowledge in the first sense is different from faith and their difference requires further analysis.

II

Science — in the widest sense — attains its objectivity by means of the concept.

A concept possesses universal meaning; it is an abstraction; like an object, it can be passed on by one person to another; with its help, men can overcome their isolation and communicate with one another. Thus, the concepts of a triangle or circle have the same objective meaning for every person.

Here we encounter one of the fundamental differences between faith and knowledge. *Faith* is the experience of the great moment; it is personal, the exclusive possession of the individual who has the experience. *Science* in all its forms is impersonal.

The value of science lies precisely in its impersonality. Science necessarily transforms the objects it investigates into abstractions. A man cannot love and at the same time subject his love to detached, uninvolved, objective analysis. In the same way, the scientist, in order to investigate the world scientifically, is compelled to deprive it of its individuality and experiential concreteness. He must disregard the fact that life pulsates in him as a man. As a scientist, he is related to the reality which he investigates and conceptualizes as an anatomist relates himself to a corpse.

Martin Buber has pointed out that not only the *object* of science but also the *subject* — the scientist *qua* scientist — is an abstraction. Science is anonymous. The biography of the scientist is irrelevant to the results of his research. His personal feelings or views do not matter; they do not affect the validity of his findings. In radical contrast, the *believer* is not anonymous. He faces God in the fullness of his existential situation; he stands before God as an individual whose deepest emotions matter, from his supreme joys to his profoundest anguish.

A second difference between faith and reason is rooted in the fact that *science is always provisional, never complete*. Science is compelled by its method to abstract concepts from reality. There is a permanent gap between our knowledge and the reality which it is meant to define and understand. Science, by its very nature, is always tentative, always "on the road," never at its end. Even if scientifically valid proofs for the existence of God could ever be formulated, they would always remain tentative and provisional precisely because they are *scientific* proofs. Pascal was right: he used to wear an amulet with the inscription, "God of Abraham, Isaac and Jacob — not the god of the philosophers." The god of the philosophers is at best a scientific hypothesis. You cannot pray to a scientific hypothesis. The Lord of Hosts wants not to be proved but to be called upon in perfect trust.

Anselm of Canterbury who was the first to formulate the ontological proof for the existence of God, is said to have implored God, prior to his discovery of the argument, to show him the way to a genuine proof. But if we wonder how Anselm could possibly have prayed to a God whose existence he had not yet been able to prove we miss the essential point. Anselm's faith did not depend on any proof. He was certain of God's existence. What he sought was a way of leading others to the same certainty. The believer needs no proof. This fact reveals both the strength as well as the weakness of faith. Unlike science, faith is not the common property of mankind; it is the exclusive possession of the individual believer. Yet to him it possesses a degree of certainty which science, by its very nature, cannot achieve.

This interpretation seems to make faith the exclusive possession of those who are fortunate enough to have what can be called a "religious experience." Granted. However, religious experiences are not the privilege of a chosen few, a divine gift capriciously bestowed upon some and withheld from others. "Seek ye the Lord while He may be found; call ye upon Him while He is near."[5] All great men of faith, in effect, testify in similar words that God can be found and faith be achieved by every person.

III

Knowledge and belief do not contradict each other; they belong to different universes of discourse. Scientific knowledge is bereft of the "I" in all its fullness; it abstracts from the concreteness of both the self and outside reality; it is objective, communicable, permanent, but forever incomplete as a process. The assumption that there is an irreconcilable conflict between knowledge and belief usually stems from a misconception of the nature of religious faith. The truth of belief cannot be formulated in verifiable propositions; religious experience does not claim that it provides answers to scientific questions. The Bible, for example, is not a primer in geology nor does it intend to teach natural science. Any concept of faith which seeks to maintain the literal "truth" of the

Biblical account of creation against the claims of geology, genetics, or archeology, is in principle meaningless and absurd.

The problem of free will versus determinism can illustrate the fact that belief and knowledge do not contradict each other. Science is deterministic by definition. Its task is to explain facts; its method of explanation is to show necessary and sufficient causes. Hence science views the universe as a machine working strictly in accordance with the principle of causality. Novelty, freedom, creativity, spontaneity, cannot be recognized; they are "uncaused" by definition and therefore inexplicable. The moment the new is explained, it is reduced to the old — and hence no longer new; the unknown is reduced to the known.

Nevertheless, we *believe* in man's freedom. Our immediate experience and certainty of our own freedom are so strong that no argument can upset them. We are persons, not blind mechanisms; we make choices which determine our actions. Otherwise men would be robots, and there would be no difference between a Shakespeare and a typewriter.

To be sure, we cannot prove man's freedom. Proof is possible only where a necessary and sufficient cause for an action or event can be shown. The choices which we make of our own free will lack such "causes" by definition. Yet the determinism of science does not refute man's belief in his freedom. The determinism of science is merely a methodological postulate. That is to say, the task of science is the analysis of the world in terms of necessary relations. But science, as we have seen, is forever incomplete: It will never be able to complete its analysis of man and his motivations. Human life cannot be reduced to a mathematical equation whose solution is wholly predictable. Hence there is no conflict between science which studies man's existence and experience in the framework of causality, and man's immediate consciousness which tells him that he is not a mere machine but a free creature, responsible for his actions.

Or consider the problem of "miracles." (The importance of this problem has been vastly exaggerated.) Here, a conflict between faith and reason seems inescapable. Faith affirms the possibility of miracles; reason must reject it. Faith claims that miracles happened in the past and may happen again. Science insists that the natural order of the universe cannot be suspended or interrupted. Miracles defy explanation by the principle of causality. Therefore they cannot happen.

But the believer needs miracles as little as he requires proof for his beliefs. It is the skeptic, not the believer, who demands miracles. The believer knows that *everything* is a miracle; everything can be conceived or experienced as a sign or message. Thus the *Siddur* says: "Thy miracles are with us day by day" and "The miracles Thou workest at all times, in the evening, the morning and at noon." To the believer, the *order* of the universe, the orderly rule of law, represents the supreme miracle. Science cannot recognize miracles; they defy the laws which govern the natural order. Nothing can be exempt from the dominion of law. But for the man of faith the miracle lies precisely in the fact that this is a universe that is governed by laws. "Man's love of miracles," said Bishop Berkeley, "is an offense to the greatest of miracles — the natural order of the world." When the believer asserts the ingression of the Divine into reality, he does not claim that a system of supernatural causality suspends the operation of the laws of causality governing nature. To him, the entire natural order manifests God's presence and power.

IV

The distinctions between faith and reason must not be obliterated. Their methods and concerns are different. Their separation, however, cannot be the last word. Their methods may differ, but the man who applies them is the same. Both represent different relationships to reality, yet they can conceivably find a deeper unity in the heart and life of the man who is both, a scientist and a man of faith. Despite the proper and necessary distinctions between faith and reason, there still remains the ideal of a world view which embodies the insights of reason yet is grounded in faith. "If," in Franz Rosenzweig's words, "science and religion attempt to ignore each other though they have knowledge of each other, both are on shaky ground. There is only one truth. No honest man can pray to a God whose existence he denies as a scientist. And he who prays cannot deny God. This does not mean that the scientist can discover God in a test-tube or historical document. But it does mean that the content of the test-tube or historical document does not exist without God. The object of science is not God but the world. But God has created the world and thus the object of science. God is transcendent but also transcendental with regard to science, that is, he makes it possible. Science does not have God for her own, yet could not be without Him. He is not a subject of science; science is subject to Him."[6]

There is no easy formula by which this synthesis between faith and reason can be achieved. There can be no distinction between a scientist who "believes" and one who does not, for as scientists both must accept the rules of scientific objectivity, i. e., of checks and controls. Profound inner struggles are involved when a man attempts to bridge and harmonize the two great poles of human existence: the *certainty* of his trust in God which he derives from his faith, and the *uncertainty* of search and detached inquiry with which, as a responsible thinker, he must subject his very assumptions to constantly renewed scrutiny. How it may be possible for us as Jews to harmonize faith and reason can best be illustrated by the thoughts and experiences of some men who were significant both as thinkers and as men of faith.

CHAPTER TWO

HERMANN COHEN: THE RELIGION OF REASON FROM THE SOURCES OF JUDAISM

Faith and reason, though mutually independent and often diametrically opposed, can be harmonized in the work and personality of the thinker who also is a man of faith. The intellectual struggle and achievements of the German-Jewish philosopher, Hermann Cohen, are a prominent illustration.

Cohen was born in Koswig in Anhalt in 1842. The son of a cantor and Hebrew teacher, he received a thorough Jewish education. He entered the Jewish Theological Seminary in Breslau in order to study for the rabbinate, but soon turned to philosophy. In 1873, he was called to the University of Marburg by Friedrich Albert Lange, the well-known author of the *History of Materialism*, and he received an appointment as full professor of philosophy after only three years of teaching. The brilliant young Jew had risen to the top of his profession at a time when the German university was at the peak of its influence and occupied a position of leadership in the intellectual life of Europe.

I

Cohen became wholly absorbed in his teaching. His Judaism was mainly a memory of his childhood experiences, not a living and lived reality. In a conversation with Lange, Cohen revealed his conviction, at that time, that liberal Christianity and Judaism differed merely in name. Lange said to him, "As far as Christianity is concerned, I presume our views differ." To this Cohen replied, "Not at all. What you call Christianity, I call prophetic Judaism."

However, in November 1879, this tranquillity was disturbed by the publication of Treitschke's pamphlet, *Ein Wort über unser Judentum*, (A Word on our Judaism). The famous historian attacked Judaism as the national religion of an alien tribe; it had nothing to offer to the German Christian in his quest for a new and purer form of Christianity. Treitschke's attack hurt Cohen deeply, and in 1880 he published a reply, *Ein Bekenntnis zur Judenfrage*, (The Jewish Question: A Confession). The introductory words show how distasteful it was for Cohen to enter this kind of controversy:

> "Once again it has become necessary that we make a public declaration of our faith. We of the younger generation had dared to hope that we would eventually succeed in becoming integrated into the nation of Immanuel Kant; that the differences that still exist would gradually disappear in an atmosphere which combines morality in political matters with a respect for historical facts; that it would become

possible to give free expression to our love of our country and to our pride in being full and equal partners in the service of our national tasks. This confidence has now been destroyed. The old anxiety has returned once more."

Cohen favored a program of deliberate assimilation in this early pamphlet. He went so far as to accept the justification of Treitschke's complaint that the Jews refuse to surrender their racial identity. Cohen wrote, "We want to amalgamate physically with the German people. There must be no double nationality, no feeling of double loyalty." But what distinguished Cohen even at that time from extreme Jewish assimilationists was the profound seriousness with which he discussed the religious aspects of the Jewish question. He demanded that the German Jews take their religion seriously precisely because of their obligation to the German people: "Respect your Hebraic monotheism; learn to understand it; preserve it in your heart, and make it the guide of your religious life." Nevertheless, Cohen still believed at that time that Judaism was essentially identical with Protestant Christianity. When a Catholic colleague, doubtful as to whether it would be proper for him to attend a celebration in honor of Martin Luther at the University of Marburg, asked Cohen how he felt about it, Cohen answered, "If I did not attend, who should?" The same views are expressed in his little book.

His position was sharply rejected by the leaders of German Jewry and the German-Jewish press. However, Cohen himself — even in the last years of his life when his attitude toward Judaism had changed radically — felt that his defense of Judaism against Treitschke's attacks had been the beginning of his return to Judaism. For he had defined the essence and uniqueness of Jewish monotheism by its emphasis on the spirituality of God and its Messianic expectation.

For the next two decades Cohen was wholly absorbed in the development of his philosophical system and took little part in public life. He spoke up, however, whenever important Jewish issues were at stake, for instance at a Talmud trial in 1888. A public school teacher in Marburg had attacked the Talmud by claiming that Jewish and especially Talmudic law governed only the relationships between Jew and Jew but not the relationships between Jews and non-Jews. The Jewish community of Marburg instituted legal proceedings against the teacher for slandering the Jewish religion. The court called in two experts, the well-known anti-Jewish Orientalist Lagarde, and Hermann Cohen, and asked them two questions: 1) Are the Talmudic laws considered binding for observant Jews and is the slandering of the Talmud, therefore, tantamount to slander of the Jewish religious community? 2) Does the Talmud state that the ethical commandments of the Mosaic law apply only to relationships between Jew and Jew but have no reference to non-Jews, who may be robbed and deceived?

The Jewish community won its case and the defendant received a short prison sentence. Cohen published his testimony under the title, *Die Nächstenliebe im*

Talmud, (Brotherly Love in the Talmud.)[1] His central concern is his attempt to establish a connection between two apparently contradictory principles of the Jewish religion: Jewish particularism and Jewish universalism; the position of Israel as the "chosen people," and the Messianic unity of all mankind. Cohen establishes the connection by conceiving God as *oheb ger*, He who loves the stranger. The vocation and task of Israel *begins* with the fact of its chosenness; but since God is conceived as He who loves the stranger, Israel's chosenness is from the very beginning directed at the unity of mankind as a whole, an ideal with whose attainment Israel's mission will end. According to Jewish thought, it is the task and purpose of history to bring about this conclusion. Greek philosophy has no concept of man as man and therefore no conception of the history of mankind. The concepts of the uniqueness and dignity of man and of the unity of mankind emerge only from the concept of the one God who has created man in His image.

World history has a goal: the Messianic Age, the realization of the kingdom of God on earth. This is the idea which now moves more and more into the foreground of Cohen's reflections on religion. Thus he writes in 1899, when he learns of the acquittal of Captain Dreyfus in France: "History is not ruled by blind chance. History reflects divine providence, a moral order. In the fate of this man, we discover and revere that providence which ennobles the individual by assigning to him the role of suffering for the sake of all. He has suffered for the Redeemer of Israel."

Cohen demands of his fellow-Jews that they, too, view Dreyfus' vindication as an act of redemption. Friends report that Cohen was in a mood of "Messianic expectation" when he received the news of the acquittal. Time and again he was moved to similar exultation by events which seemed to reveal traces of Messianic fulfillment. He possessed what Nathan Birnbaum once described as "Messianic seriousness" (*Messias-Ernst*) which, for Birnbaum, characterizes the authentic Jew. Plato had held that the world would never be free from evil. Cohen differs from Plato, his revered teacher. Messianism means the assurance that injustice *will* ultimately disappear. "Nothing can destroy this confidence. Neither skepticism nor pessimism; neither mysticism nor metaphysics; neither our knowledge of the evil men can do nor the harsh realities of life can demolish it. Reality is not condemned forever to remain the mere shadow of the ideal. The gap between ideal and reality is neither absolute nor eternal; it can and will be bridged by the Messiah."

The fervor of Cohen's faith in the possibility and nearness of Messianic fulfillment is revealed by a touching story of a conversation which Franz Rosenzweig had with Cohen who then was already past seventy. "Cohen said to me: 'Even I hope yet to see the arrival of the Messianic age.' I was deeply stirred by this powerful affirmation of the '*Soon*, *in our time*,' but could only comment hesitatingly that I myself, though many years younger, did not expect to live that long. 'But what is your guess?' asked Cohen. I did not dare mention a figure and said vaguely, 'In a hundred years perhaps,' whereupon Cohen took my hand and said, 'Oh, please, make it fifty.'"

Cohen defined the Messianic Age primarily in terms of a philosophic socialism which firmly rejected historical materialism. The struggle for the Messianic kingdom is a struggle for justice and the rights of the poor. And the idea of God signifies the assurance and indeed the guarantee that this struggle will end victoriously with the establishment of the kingdom of God.

When Cohen was invited in 1910 to speak at the World Congress for Religious Progress on "The Importance of Judaism for the Religious Progress of Mankind," he summarized the essence of Judaism in six points:

1. The special characteristic of Judaism is that it emphasizes not merely the unity of God but above all His uniqueness; that is, His absolute difference from all creatures. Thus, pantheism is rejected.
2. In Judaism, man confronts God directly. No intermediary, be he a priest or a God-man, is required.
3. There is an indissoluble relationship between knowledge and belief in Judaism. Study is a sacred duty. Hence Judaism knows no conflict between faith and knowledge.
4. The importance of the Sabbath.
5. The Jewish emphasis on freedom and moral responsibility of the individual, and the rejection of the concept of original sin.
6. The concept that history has a direction and a goal: the Messianic unity of mankind.

Cohen sees the essence and distinctiveness of Judaism in these six points. Thirty years after his controversy with Treitschke, his position has changed radically. He no longer maintains that Judaism and Christianity have a fundamental similarity. He emphasizes their differences sharply by rejecting the concepts of a mediator and of original sin as utterly incompatible with Judaism.

II

We have briefly sketched Cohen's first publications in the field of Judaism. To understand his later Jewish development and especially his synthesis of faith and reason, we must now turn to his system and to the teachings of the "Marburg School" which he founded.

Cohen's system is a consistent, radical idealism which teaches that being is wholly rooted in reason. Here Cohen goes far beyond the teaching of his master, Kant. For Kant certainly also thought that reason constructs the world; but the materials out of which the world is formed are, according to Kant, our sense impressions. They are "given" to us, not produced by us. In the Kantian system, thought is a synthesis, the creation of connection between the sense impressions which are given.

For Cohen, thought produces everything out of itself. He rejects the notion that thought has merely a synthesizing function while drawing its material from sensation. According to Cohen, sensation merely describes the problem posed to thought. Sensation demands something, it signifies a claim, but it cannot satisfy this claim from its own resources. Pure thought must come to its aid.

For example, the scale of colors and sounds discovered by physics far exceeds the limits set to our eyes and ears. Our knowledge of reality is therefore based on sensation to such a small extent that the theories of physics are not at all confirmed by sensation. "Sensation stammers; thought must first supply the word; sensation denotes the dark impulse; but only thought can illuminate its direction."

Thus thought "constructs" the world of objects. With this notion, Cohen introduces his fundamental "principle of origin" which emphasizes the sovereignty of thought. Thought "produces" its object. The objects of thought are of course not identical with the "things" in our daily life. The scientific object, the electron for example, is constituted by the network of laws and inter-relations of science. To the chemist the water we drink is H_2O. Because the object is defined and constituted by scientific thought as the epitome of certain relationships, it is unambiguous and identical in quite a different way than are the objects of daily life.

The three great systematic works of Cohen bear the titles *Logic of Pure Knowledge* (1902), *Ethics of Pure Will* (1904), *Aesthetics of Pure Feeling* (1912). The word "pure" is present in all three titles. We use the term pure wine when it is free from all admixture. In the same way, Cohen speaks of pure knowledge in order to indicate that it is free from any admixture with sense experience. Cohen once gave a paradoxical description of this idealistic and pure "principle of origin" when he said of the stars: "It is not in the heavens that the stars are fixed but in the science of astronomy."

This sentence enables us to understand Cohen's view on the relationship of philosophy to science and to culture in general. The astronomer at first proceeds "naively," without philosophic reflection. He begins with the stars and their movements as they are given to his senses. But the progress of his research forces him to emancipate himself more and more from the senses, to correct the data of sensations, to replace the sensible world by a world of conceptual construction. It is now that philosophy appears — in this case the logic and theory of knowledge — and asks: What are the presuppositions on which the astronomer based his research? The philosopher will discover that two tendencies are at work in science: certain presuppositions are laid down as basic principles and the facts are determined with their help; but the progress of science, in turn, requires a revision of the principles originally laid down as fundamental. New hypotheses are established which, in turn, lead to the discovery of new "facts." The process of knowledge is infinite, forever growing yet forever incomplete.

Only the search for truth matters. No final, absolute truth can exist for man since the process of science is infinite. "Reality is never reached; it is an infinite task that is never attained, the final goal of a journey that is never completed." Solomon Maimon had given a similar interpretation of Kantian philosophy two generations before Cohen.[2] And when Cohen's contemporary, the socialist Eduard Bernstein, in a discussion of socialist tactics, said, "The way is everything, the goal is nothing," one can discover the influence of the Marburg school on contemporary thought. Reality is volatilized in favor of abstraction, the final goal in favor of the method of its attainment.

III

Ethics is for Cohen the theory of *man*. It does, of course, not treat man as a zoological specimen, as *homo sapiens*. The difference between ethics and other branches of knowledge lies in the fact that disciplines such as zoology and psychology know and treat man only as an individual. Ethics, however, does not take cognizance of man as an individual, as man-by-himself; it knows him only as a link in the totality of men. In his introduction to Lange's *History of Materialism*, Cohen terms it "presumptuous" to raise *ethical* questions concerning man as an individual. This is not the task of philosophy but of disciplines such as medicine or psychology. But this presumptuousness can be effectively refuted only from a standpoint already established by Plato — that man as an object of ethics is neither rooted in nature nor an individual being at all, but that he is, from the very beginning, an abstraction who acquires concrete existence only through his membership in the *community of men*. This community passes through manifold stages (clan, tribe, nations, etc.) before it reaches its culmination in humanity as a whole. This view is the fundamental principle of Cohen's ethics for which he is indebted to Kant. For Kant's "categorical imperative" (in which my act must be judged in terms of whether all men may properly do it) emphasized the very fact that before the judgment seat of ethics the individual is a representative of humanity which is incorporated in him as in every other individual.

IV

There is no place for religion in Cohen's Marburg system. For his system, as we have just seen, is established on a definition of culture as the free creation of man, resting on foundations laid down by man himself. But the central categories of religion, at least of the Jewish religion, — creation, revelation, covenant, sin, repentance, return — cannot be understood as mere hypothetical assumptions made by man if the meaning of religion is not to be utterly destroyed. The concepts of religion claim an absoluteness, a truth not just in reason but in the universe itself, which the system of the Marburg school, with its emphasis on the spontaneity and creative act of man, cannot acknowledge.

Cohen himself, in this period of his development, justifies the absence of religion from his concept of culture by a formal argument. The three fields of culture — knowledge, politics, art — correspond to the three basic modes in which consciousness manifests itself: thinking, willing, feeling. There is no fourth separate and independent mode of consciousness which can serve as the foundation for a specifically religious field of culture. Kant still had been able to assign a place of its own to religion and had not dissolved it completely into ethics. Cohen rejects this position. "Ethics simply cannot acknowledge the independence of religion." It can, therefore, acknowledge religion only as a primitive stage in its own development, a transitional phenomenon which disappears when ethics reaches its maturity.

But though there is no place for religion as such in Cohen's early thinking, he assigns an important place to the *concept* of God in his system. In 1872, still as a young man, Cohen had written to his friend, Hermann Lewandowsky: "Every endeavor in ethics which is made without God is bereft of thought and principle." In his great ethical work of 1904, the idea of God is introduced as the bridge which links the natural sciences and morality. Ethics places an eternal ideal before us, but science can give us no guarantee that the world of nature in which we live will exist eternally. On the contrary, it maintains that the world will perish after millions of years. If this prediction materializes, what will become of morality? There is a "gap in the methodology of fundamental ideas" as long as the permanence of nature and of man in nature are not assured. It is inconceivable for Cohen that the world should come to an end for physical reasons before the goal of morality, the Messianic Age, has been achieved.

It is at this point that Cohen introduces the "idea" of God into his system. The idea of God provides the guarantee that there will always exist a nature and a human race through which moral progress can be achieved. "God means that the duration of nature is guaranteed as surely as morality is eternal." To support his approach, Cohen quotes the story of God's covenant with Noah (Genesis 9.15) which guarantees that mankind will never again be destroyed by a natural catastrophe. Physical reality constituted by natural science, and morality founded on ethical reason can ultimately not remain separate realms; ultimately, nature will be the setting for the complete realization of the ethical ideal.

Cohen's concept of God is the product of his philosophical rationalism. He offers no "proof" for God's existence in the classical tradition of philosophy. He does not speak of God's "being" but of the "idea" of God. This idea is merely a hypothesis, a concept developed by the philosopher. God does not "exist"; He has no "reality." As an idea, He cannot be described nor does He have to be "believed" in. He can be discovered by the processes of reason itself. The idea of God is introduced by Cohen in order "to preserve nature for ethics," to assure the maintenance of the physical world for the moral ideal.

This abstract notion of God has little in common with the God of Judaism. In a letter written in 1907,

Cohen reveals that he is aware of this dilemma: "I have a fate of a peculiar sort. Others may sacrifice their intellect. I must sacrifice my emotions. As you know, my heart and my feelings respond deeply to the emotional aspects of our religion; but abstraction is my fate."[3] The extent to which Cohen feels he has to sacrifice his emotions is reflected in an anecdote reported by Franz Rosenzweig: "When Cohen still lived in Marburg, he once explained to an old Jew the idea of God which he had developed in his ethics. The old man listened attentively, but when Cohen had finished he asked him: 'But where is the *bore olam*, the creator of the world?' Cohen did not reply a single word, but there were tears in his eyes."

We are confronted by a moving tension. Cohen longs for the living God of Israel and, like Abraham, wants to say, "Here I am." But his emotions conflict with the demands of his intellectual consistency. His philosophical idealism demands the complete autonomy of the self, dependent only on reason and the moral law within, both man's own possessions. Whatever else there is must have its roots and origin in these sources. Hence Cohen, in his Marburg period, is compelled to refuse to recognize not only an autonomous world but also an autonomous God. Only the self can be autonomous.

One of the intellectual leaders of orthodox Judaism in Germany[4] criticized Cohen for transforming the living God of Israel into a mere philosophical idea. The reproach is justified but does not do justice to Cohen's severe inner struggles and his insistence on intellectual integrity. In remaining true to his philosophical idealism, Cohen is compelled to replace the living God of his fathers with the "idea" of the realization of morality in the Messianic Age; God is an idea, the creation of the human mind. "Beyond that, it is meaningless." Religion is dissolved into ethics, and in its very capacity for being dissolved into ethics Cohen finds the ultimate value of religion.

However, in assigning a central position to the idea of God within the system of ethics itself, Cohen is more emphatic than any previous philosopher in his insistence that the idea of God is indispensable to any mature system of ethics.

Judaism's significance and greatness, for Cohen, reside precisely in its complete identification of the prophetic concept of God with morality. Thus he writes to the B'nai B'rith Lodge of Frankfurt which had sent him a letter of felicitation on the publication of his *Ethics*;

> ". . . . It is very encouraging that the relationships between knowledge in general and the knowledge of Judaism are noticed and evoke a gratifying response. You suggest correctly that a man has the duty to be truthful; and it is precisely this duty which demands an appreciation of Judaism in my ethical system. My enthusiasm for Judaism is rooted in my conviction of the profound ethical value which our idea of God possesses; my Judaism is intimately related to my philosophical insights. Therefore I am particularly happy that I was able to show the significance of Judaism within the context of a philosophic system before daring to treat it in its

own right. In this respect, I have entrusted the guidance of my Jewish consciousness not to a mere tribal instinct or sense of blind loyalty, but to the control of a strict philosophical method."[5]

Nevertheless, at this stage of his development Cohen penetrates merely to the *idea* of God, not to God Himself. And the idea of God is a creation of man's reason, in complete contra-distinction to the claims of the religious mind for which man is the creation of a living and existing God. For Cohen, man's reason is logically prior to God; it *posits* the idea of God as its own ultimate ideal, the ideal of Messianic mankind.

V

In 1912, Cohen retired from the University of Marburg and moved to Berlin. The move was more than a change of residence. He became increasingly preoccupied with Jewish affairs and the fundamental religious concepts of Judaism. He lectured on the great Jewish philosophers and especially on his favorite, Maimonides, at the *Hochschule für die Wissenschaft des Judentums*. At the beginning of 1914 he travelled to Russian Poland where a *numerus clausus* limited the number of Jews entering high school. Cohen's hope was to counteract the effects of this measure by organizing an independent network of schools for Russian Jewry. His personal contact with the Jewish masses in Vilna and Warsaw, together with the almost triumphal reception given him by Jewish and Russian intellectuals impressed him profoundly.

These years brought a radical change in Cohen's philosophic orientation. He himself was never fully aware of it but its first signs became evident when he published a new book in 1915, *Der Begriff der Religion im System der Philosophie*. The title of the volume, *The Concept of Religion Within the System of Philosophy*, in itself reveals the change in Cohen's basic position. No special place had originally been left for religion in the Marburg system. Now, in his first book after leaving Marburg — dedicated "to the Marburg School in gratitude and trust" — Cohen seeks an autonomous place for the concept of religion in his system. His concern arises from the discovery of a problem which cannot be mastered by ethics alone: the problem of the individual.

Ethics, as Cohen understands it, cannot take cognizance of the individual *qua* individual. It must treat everyone alike; it cannot make any distinction between one man and another. It must be indifferent to the personal and intimate problems of man as an individual. It has no room for his sin and anguish, his repentance or need of salvation. The salvation of the individual is the true task of religion. It is religion which is concerned with the individual man. In contrast to his earlier views, Cohen now finds a distinct place for religion.

The indifference of ethics vis-à-vis the individual is evidenced by another factor. Ethics is not interested in the success of the moral deed. Its sole concern is the moral act itself, not its success or failure. It is certain of its final victory, but it can patiently wait thousands of years. The individual's victory or failure are unimportant to ethics. But they are a profound concern to religion. Religion, says Cohen, "objects to this fiction of indifference. It must not remain a matter of unconcern whether my morality and the morality of mankind are only a performance of our duty; I must also ask whether the ideal [toward which I strive] has life and reality." Now the God who is the subject of religious teaching "signifies the removal of the presupposition that morality is only law and commandment but never human reality."

Thus it was religion, not ethics, which discovered the individual. Cohen ascribes this discovery to the later prophets. The earlier, "social" prophets, like Amos, Isaiah and Micah, judged the world from the ethical standpoint alone and knew the individual only as a member of the group, subject to the laws of the community. They envisioned a united humanity and were concerned with the history of states and societies, not with the individual and his sufferings. Only the later prophets, especially Jeremiah[6] and above all Ezekiel, discovered the individual. Ezekiel sharply rejected the notion that the children must suffer for the sins of their fathers; by discovering sin to be the burden of the individual, Ezekiel discovered the concept of the individual as such.[7]

Notions such as sin, repentance and forgiveness are not ethical but religious categories. Cohen, who in his earlier period had evaluated religion by its capacity to be absorbed into ethics, now castigates the "social" prophets for not having given sufficient emphasis to the distinctiveness of religion vis-à-vis morality.

Cohen's new thinking finds its fullest expression and final form in his great book, *Die Religion der Vernunft aus den Quellen des Judentums* (Religion of Reason from the Sources of Judaism), which his wife published after his death in 1918. [Martha Cohen was the daughter of the famous cantor and composer, Louis Lewandowski, to whom the Jewish liturgy owes much of its sacred music.]

VI

Die Religion der Vernunft aus den Quellen des Judentums reveals the radical change which has occurred in Cohen's thinking. In his Marburg period, he saw reality rooted in human reason and culture as the product of the human mind. In his Berlin period, all reality is rooted in God and both, man and his reason originate in God. God is radically reconceived. He no longer is "becoming," a mere postulate, the ideal of Messianic mankind to which reason forever aspires. He is pure being — "I am that I am" — relative to which everything else is non-being.

Because God and only He is being, He is "unique" (*einzig*). In his lecture on "The Importance of Judaism for the Religious Progress of Humanity" in 1910, Cohen had already stressed the decisive importance of the concept of God's unity:

"It is necessary to understand the particular character of Jewish monotheism. 'Unity' here means absolute uniqueness. And this means absolute otherness, distinct not only from all material but also from all other spiritual being. Only in this way is the one being of the one God endowed with true spirituality. This one-sidedness belongs to the essence of the Jewish conception of God. As God has a being different from all other being, He represents true being compared with which all being of nature and of the quality of man itself is mere appearance and shadow."

Paul Lagarde, Cohen's opponent in the Marburg trial, had argued that, in Judaism, the difference between monotheism and polytheism was only arithmetical and did not justify any claim to pre-eminence on the part of Judaism. In Cohen's view, the uniqueness of God implies not simply a numerical oneness but signifies the radical distinction between God and creation which characterizes Jewish monotheism and protects it against any pantheistic dilution.

There is a radical ontological difference between God and all finite, creaturely existence. God is being, the world is becoming and process. Cohen's Marburg system knows only of "becoming" and does not penetrate to "being". Now the problem is reversed: not being but becoming is the problem. How can anything which is by nature finite and incomplete and hence eternally in process exist side by side with God? This is the central problem which now occupies Cohen's mind.

Cohen attempts to resolve the problem by introducing a new concept, the concept of "correlation." *Being* and *becoming* belong together. They are correlative to each other; one requires the other logically. "Becoming," — the finite, created world which is constantly in process and change — cannot exist unless it is contained and originates in "being" which gives it power and significance. But being also cannot exist without becoming. For God's being has no meaning without creation through which He manifests Himself. Creation is the logical consequence of God's unique being. There is no mankind without God, but there can also be no God without mankind. "The basic framework of religious knowledge is established in the correlation between God and man."[8]

This new basic framework of Cohen's religious thought has several implications. For Cohen, the Biblical concept of the creation of man in the image of God means that man's reason is created by God. In support of this interpretation, Cohen quotes Zechariah 12.1, "God formeth the spirit of man within him," and Job 31.2, describing the spirit of man as "the portion of God from above and the inheritance of the Almighty from on high."

Cohen's turn from his former views is radical and profound. The "principle of origin" of the Marburg system makes human reason the creator of the whole of culture, and every concept of culture including the idea of God has to vindicate itself before the tribunal of human reason. Now human reason is no longer the ultimate tribunal, the autonomous origin of everything else. God is the origin and He has created man's soul in His image. Human reason no longer reigns supreme; it has yielded its place to Him who alone is entitled to rule. Cohen's system has shifted from an anthropocentric to a theocentric orientation.

But his theocentrism is bound up with the principle of correlation. His starting point is the basic duality of God and man; the other basic dualities — of God and world and of man and man — emerge from it. Thus Cohen, in Rosenzweig's words, "advanced with a powerful surge far beyond the philosophical country of the future," into the philosophy of dialogue, represented on the Jewish side by Franz Rosenzweig and Martin Buber. Cohen's road from idealism to the system of correlation — in other words, from the ego to the I-Thou relationship — anticipates the intellectual development of a whole epoch and becomes its model.

The correlation between God and man is characterized by what the Jewish tradition calls *ruaḥ hakodesh*, the Spirit of Holiness. This "holy spirit" is *between* man and God, not *in* either. It is not an attribute of either God or man, but of their relation.

For this reason, Cohen criticizes Philo and Christianity; instead of seeing that the Holy Spirit is the spirit of holiness which characterizes the *relationship* between God and man, they hypostasize the "Holy Spirit" as an independent substance and separate divine entity mediating between God and man. "The Greek spirit which is the epitome of scientific worldliness seeks for mediation, as they put it, between God and man. The Jew Philo with his logos fell victim to this Greek enchantment."[9]

The Holy Spirit binds God to man and man to God, yet both remain distinct from each other. God does not become man, nor does man become God. The principle of correlation prevents their distinction from becoming separation; on the contrary, it brings about their connection. "Holiness in God would be pointless if it did not find its practical application in man." Men fulfill their striving for holiness in acknowledging God as the model and source of holiness.

This reciprocity reveals a new and important aspect of correlation, the collaboration of God and man. Correlation is the narrow ridge between two dangerous abysses: man's activism, his trust in his own power, his confidence that heaven is not needed (this was the view of the atheistic humanism of the nineteenth century), and an attitude exemplified, for instance, by Luther who makes man the passive recipient (or non-recipient) of divine grace. Man's own activity is unimportant and of no concern. Cohen, in rejecting both extremes, follows the tradition of classical Jewish thought. Man is bound to God through the "covenant" of correlation; in the words of the Talmud, he is a "co-worker in the work of creation," yet ultimately powerless without grace from above. That correlation demands both man's deed and divine grace is illustrated by two verses of Ezekiel, quoted by Cohen, where the salvation of man, his "new heart," is described both as the deed of repentant man himself and as the work of God: "Cast away from you all transgressions, whereby ye have transgressed; and *make* you a new heart and a new spirit" (18.31) and "A new heart also will I *give* you, and a new spirit will I put within you" (36.26). Both are true and both are required. Man must turn to God in repentance. But man's return to God must find its consummation in God's forgiveness of man's sin.

Thus man has a share in the work of creation by virtue of his correlation with God. Man's specific creative responsibility is the establishment of the one, Messianic mankind. A united mankind cannot be the product of nature; nature created "man" but not "mankind." It knows only one man *beside* the other (*Nebenmensch*), persons living side by side, not *with* one another. Their natural relationship is aptly characterized by the saying, "Man is a wolf to man." Man's task, however, is to transform this natural relationship into an ethical relationship, natural man into fellow-man (*Mitmensch*). Man's creation by nature is to be completed by a second act of creation, man's re-creation of himself.

The one united humanity does not yet exist. Its realization requires the existence of communities in which the sense of mutuality and responsibility which characterizes the ethical relationship between man and his fellow-man is a living reality. Models, symbols, or rather cells of the humanity of the future are required. To Hermann Cohen, Israel is such a "symbol of humanity." The Greeks did not possess such a symbol for they lacked the very concept of mankind. The idea of one mankind is founded on the affirmation of the one God, and the concept of one God arose only in Israel.

VII

The *Religion der Vernunft aus den Quellen des Judentums* has been described as the great gift of liberal Judaism to Jewish theology. Cohen was indeed a liberal Jew, but he accepted and vigorously affirmed the value and significance of Jewish tradition and law. *Mitzvah* means both "law" and "duty". The law originates in God, the sense of duty in man. The law is at the same time duty, duty, at the same time law. God issues commandments to man and man, of his own free will, takes this "yoke of the commandments" upon himself; but with the "yoke of the commandments" he simultaneously accept the "yoke of the kingdom of God." Again the law leads to the Messianic idea of mankind.

Cohen had genuine respect for the meaning and significance of tradition, custom and ceremony. His attitude is illustrated by his views on the place of the Hebrew language in the religious life of the Jew. Cohen is convinced that it is necessary to conduct at least part of the religious service in the vernacular. "Prayer is the language of the heart; but the language of the heart is one's mother tongue." At the same time, he warns against radicalism and excesses and urges his fellow-Jews to acquire sufficient command of Hebrew to enable them to understand the Bible and the Prayer Book in the original. Prayer, too, "must be used as a means of teaching the content of belief, of emphasizing the most important religious ideas, of serving as an introduction to the spirit of religion."

This goal requires the use of the original text. A translation inevitably introduces an alien spirit into the original Biblical thought. Thus, the Christian translation of the term "*ehad*" as "*one*" fails to express the uniqueness of God. The same is true of every term whose Christian meaning differs from the Jewish. "Redemption," "the shepherd," "the lamb which is led to slaughter" — all these are terms which have a different connotation and feeling tone for the Christian than they have for the Jew. "There is . . . no other remedy but to let the original language express the original idea and feeling. It is instructive to note that many Jews are no longer aware of the fact that 'Redeemer' is of Jewish origin. Our general culture knows it merely as a Christian term. . . . Or think of the wealth of spiritual values and treasures which our Jewish prayers contain. . . . Innumerable Biblical passages are woven into them. . . . The spiritual power of prayer is tied to the power of language; our ideas have emerged in this language and the feelings and connotations which they evoke cannot be separated from it. The congregation administers a vital treasure in the prayers of tradition. Its core must remain untouched in order to bring out the unique religious thoughts and feelings which are latent in it."

In calling for a living relationship to the Hebrew language, Cohen expresses his concern not only for the Jew and his religion but also for his Christian environment. For the specific Jewish contribution to the general culture in which the Jew lives consists in the perpetual creative revitalization of his religious life. "All of Christian culture is permeated by the spirit of the Old Testament. The noblest figures of poetry . . . . stem from it or are enriched by it. . . . Hence it is wrong to consider the stress on Hebrew an isolation from the language of the surrounding culture. On the contrary. Through its channels we can receive new nourishment from the ancient wellspring which will open up again."

VIII

This, then, is the spiritual biography of Hermann Cohen, one of the significant Jewish thinkers of our time. His starting point is the proud position of idealistic philosophy: culture is the creation of the human spirit alone. Reason is autonomous. It cannot permit itself to receive or accept anything from another source, be it sense experience or a transcendent God and His revelation. In such a system, Cohen must look in vain for a place for God and must reluctantly be satisfied with an abstraction, the *idea* of a God, who is identified with the ideal of Messianic mankind. But in his old age the inner revolution takes place which is characteristic of his second period. Now the core of reality is God, the sole and unique being, the Creator who has fashioned man in His image. Human reason is no longer the source and origin of reality. According to the word of Job, reason partakes of God: it is *created* reason. In Cohen's early period, reason can find no place for faith; now faith encompasses reason as part of itself.

Chapter Three

FRANZ ROSENZWEIG: BEYOND LIBERALISM AND ORTHODOXY

Hermann Cohen secured the independence of religion from ethics by pointing out that ethics deals only with man in general while religion is concerned with man as an individual. Franz Rosenzweig's philosophy has its inception in this very distinction; its heart is the recognition of the central position of the individual as a concrete, particular, existing self. Even in Rosenzweig's time this type of philosophy was already known as "existentialist" though the term was not yet as fashionable and over-used as it is today. Since Rosenzweig's philosophy and theology are based on the centrality of the individual, his own biography offers an excellent key to their understanding.[1]

Franz Rosenzweig was born in Kassel, Germany, on December 25, 1886, the only son of a well-to-do Jewish merchant. He began to study medicine but shifted, after several years, to the study of history and philosophy at the University of Freiburg where he earned his doctorate in 1912 with his work on *Hegel and the State*. The year before the First World War he spent in Berlin where he heard Cohen lecture at the *Hochschule*. Cohen and Rosenzweig became close friends. During the war, he served as a volunteer with the artillery, mainly in the Balkans. He wrote his great work, *The Star of Redemption*, on the battlefield, on post cards which he sent to his parents for safekeeping. After the war, he completed the work and published it in 1921.

The Star of Redemption is an attempt at a Jewish theology. No attempt of similar magnitude had been made in the field of Jewish theology since the great theologians of the middle of the nineteenth century — Solomon Steinheim, S. R. Hirsch, Ben Amosegh and their contemporaries — had published their systems; Cohen's posthumous work had not yet appeared when Rosenzweig wrote his book. Here was the son of a wealthy businessman, brought up without any relationship to Jewish life and values, in his youth concerned mostly with art and music, utterly disinterested in Jewish life and affairs — what made this man write a book on Jewish theology? It emerged from a ten-year development as dramatic as that of any young Jew of our time.

Two letters which he wrote to his parents in 1909 show the first traces of his determination to regard matters of faith with utmost seriousness. Hans Ehrenberg, a cousin of his, had become converted to Christianity. Rosenzweig's parents wrote to Franz that they had been deeply shocked by their nephew's defection which they considered a disgrace. Their reaction distressed Franz. He answered that he himself had advised this step. Hans had felt in need of a living religion — something which his parents had completely failed to give him. Was it not better "to repair the omission belatedly than not at all? Because I am hungry, must I go on being hungry on principle? Does principle satisfy a hunger? Can being non-religious, on principle, satisfy a religious need? Or can the empty notation in the registrar's office, 'Religion: Jewish', satisfy a religious need? If I am given the choice between an empty purse and a handful of money, must I choose the purse — again on principle?" "We are Christians in everything. We live in a Christian state, attend Christian schools, read Christian books, in short, our whole culture rests entirely on Christian foundations. Therefore, where a man possesses nothing that holds him back, he needs only a very slight push . . . . to make him accept Christianity."

Judaism has become an "empty purse," Rosenzweig charges, because the Jewish home has failed. It would be absurd to blame the religious school. "Formal religious education is of no avail in the absence of the *reality* of religion — a religion seen with the eye, tasted with the mouth, heard by the ear, in short, practiced physically."

Of such a living religion Rosenzweig himself had seen little at home, and his close friends and relatives — Eugen Rosenstock, Rudolf and Hans Ehrenberg — nothing at all. Rosenstock wrote to Rosenzweig: "Like yours, my parental home, with the best of intentions, worships enlightenment and 'culture' and is Jewishly in a state of disintegration." Rosenzweig wrote something similar to his mother who though very close to him considered herself sufficiently "enlightened" to regard a religious person as a queer phenomenon: "Do you not adopt this attitude because of a deliberate and consistent disregard of all reality which lies beyond the purview of the *Frankfurter Zeitung*?"

Genuine faith seemed beyond the grasp of the *Frankfurter Zeitung* and of the educated middle-class Jew in the Germany of that time. Strangely enough, a group of young people between 25 and 30 came to sense this lack of a religious faith so keenly that they finally felt compelled to reconstruct their personal world and lives in terms of a religious faith. Rosenzweig was the only member of the group who hesitated for some time to take this step. Rooted in the philosophy of German idealism; immersed in the world of Schelling and Hegel, he struggled for some time against the leap from his position of philosophical idealism into faith. He finally surrendered in a decisive conversation with Rosenstock on July 7, 1913: "The fact that a man like Rosenstock could be a conscientious Christian revolutionized my whole conception not only of Christianity but also of religion generally and hence of my own." Together with this entire group of young Jews, Rosenzweig was ready to reject the Europe of his time, to turn his back on the world of the *Frankfurter Zeitung*, and to enter the world of religious faith. Eugen Rosenstock expressed their inner development and rebellion in his sharp criticism of Goethe who, in his *Faust*, had proclaimed the new gospel of European man by replacing the Gospel passage, "In the Beginning was the Word," with the dictum, "In the Beginning was the Deed." Rosenstock denounced this change as "Goethe's frog perspective, insensitive to the stars, a system as limited and palpable as it is coldly objective and soulless."[2] In the beginning was the *word of God*, not the *deed of man*.

This is the conviction at which Rosenzweig had finally arrived. A union of faith and reason is possible. "An intellectual's attitude toward the world and history can be one of religious faith."[3] He has discovered faith, and his turning to faith is accompanied by a profound inner change. "Only now I know," he writes, "what life really is and what it means to live with people. But the burdens of life, too, I had not known either until now."

II

Rosenzweig has become a man of faith. But what kind of faith? Eugen Rosenstock and his cousins Ehrenberg had claimed that Judaism had withered away, that it was dead, unable to quench the thirst of the seeker after faith. They had embraced Christianity and Rudolf Ehrenberg had become a Protestant minister. No one doubted that Rosenzweig who had been won over to faith by these men, would follow their example. How can one accept *faith* without at the same time *love*, the love of Jesus Christ? Only in one point Rosenzweig remains adamant. He will come to Christianity neither as a pagan nor as a non-believer but as a *Jew*. To his friends, Judaism may be dead; to him, it still is very much alive. Therefore he will become a convert in the sense in which the *Epistle to the Hebrew* speaks of the ultimate conversion of the entire Jewish people: he will follow the path advocated by the Christian missionaries to the Jews and keep the law until the very moment of conversion, in the view of the Church, releases the Jew from his obligation to observe the *mitzvot*.

During the following weeks Rosenzweig lived through profound inner conflicts. Finally, eleven weeks after his fateful night-long conversation with Rosenstock, he wrote to his cousin, Pastor Ehrenberg:

> "Dear Rudi: I must tell you something that will grieve you and may at first seem incomprehensible to you. After prolonged and, I believe, thorough self-examination, I have reversed my decision. It no longer seems necessary to me and hence — in my case — no longer possible. I shall remain a Jew."[4]

Rosenzweig's decision was a turning point not only for his own life but also for Judaism and for the perennial and still unfinished dialogue between Judaism and Christianity.

His formulation is significant: "It is no longer necessary." He clarified and expanded the point in a later letter:[5]

> "Shall I become converted, *elected* as I am from birth? Christianity's task is to convert the *pagans*. It converts them to Jesus Christ, who, for them, is the road to the Father. For the Jew, however, this road is an unnecessary detour. He is chosen from birth; from the moment of his birth on he is with the Father while the church will reach him only at

the end of time. Christianity acknowledges the God of Judaism, not, however, as God but as the 'Father of Jesus Christ.' Christianity cleaves to Jesus because it knows that the Father can be reached only through him. Jesus Christ will remain the Lord of his church until the end of days; only then will he, too, become subject to the Father who will then be the sole Lord of all. You and I are agreed as to what Christ and his church mean to the world: no one can come to the Father save through him.

"No one can *come* to the Father! This excludes him who no longer has to come to the Father because he already is with Him. This is the case with the people of Israel (though perhaps not with individual Jews). Chosen by the Father, the people of Israel has fixed its gaze across the world and history upon that last, most distant point when He, Israel's own Father, will be the One and Only One, 'all in all.' At the very moment when Christ ceases to be the Lord for the church, Israel will cease to be chosen. On that day, God will lose the name by which only Israel has been calling Him; he will no longer be the 'God of Israel'.

"Until that eternal day dawns, the life work of Israel is to anticipate it in profession and action, to be its living herald, to be a 'nation of priests' which, in fulfilling God's law, hallows His name through its own holiness. What the position of this people of God in the world is; how it has set itself apart from the world and, as a result, has taken upon itself the anguish of persecutions from without and of spiritual rigidity, of petrifaction from within — on this we are wholly agreed.

"But the synagogue accepts the anguish of denying the world for the sake of the same ultimate hope that impels the church to submit to the anguish of affirming the world. . . . Since their expectations — the God who is the God of all times — are rooted in a common ground and the revelation of the Old Covenant is common to both church and synagogue, they depend on each other.

"The synagogue which is immortal but stands with broken staff and blindfolded, must renounce all work in this world and muster all her strength to preserve her life and keep herself unsullied by life. Thus she leaves all work in the world to the church and recognizes it as the instrument for the salvation of the heathen for all times. The synagogue knows and admits that what the works of law and ritual do for Israel, the works of love do for the world outside of Israel. But the synagogue refuses to admit that the power with which the church performs her works of love, is a power that is derived from God Himself. Here the synagogue continues to look unwaveringly into the future.

"And the church, with its unbreakable staff and her eyes open to the world, this champion always certain of victory, faces the perennial danger of succumbing to the laws of the vanquished heathens. . . ."[6]

III

Rosenzweig's views, — he later expanded them in his correspondence with Eugen Rosenstock and in his *Star of Redemption*, — are of decisive importance for the dialogue between Judaism and Christianity. *Judaism and Christianity are both authentic manifestations of the one religious truth.* This thesis is wholly new and without precedent in the history of Jewish theology.

Ernst Simon has pointed out that Jewish theology has usually taken cognizance of Christianity only in a spirit of apologetics and asserted that only Judaism possesses absolute truth while Christianity possesses at best a partial truth, while many of its doctrines are in error. Rosenzweig's work actually "is the first attempt in Jewish theological thought to understand Judaism and Christianity as equally 'true' and valid views of reality."[7] Both are truly revealed religions yet each one, in itself, possesses only part of the truth. For to man, truth must always remain partial. The full truth is only with God.

Rosenzweig himself did not consider his approach to Christianity as anything new. For him, truth is vouchsafed, at least partially, not only to the Jews but to all peoples. He supports his view by quoting a legend of Jewish tradition which tells that the Messiah was born at the very moment when the Temple was destroyed. However, the winds carried him off immediately. Since then he has been wandering from one nation to the other, unknown and unrecognized. Only after he has been among all of them, will the time for our redemption come.

Despite Rosenzweig's disclaimer, the fact remains that his concept of Christianity is something new in the history of Jewish thought precisely because, to him, Christianity is not a partial truth which will ultimately be superseded when the truth of Judaism is universally accepted. Both have equally important roles to perform in the divine economy; and both will have completed their task and disappear *at the end of time* when their partial truths will be superseded by the disclosure of God's full truth. In *history*, their vocations differ. Judaism is the fire, or the *eternal life*; Christianity is the rays emanating from the fire, or the *eternal way*. "The mission of Judaism is to endure till the end of the world as the people of the King before Whom one day all the nations will bow down. The mission of Christianity is to preach to the heathen, to christianize the countries of the world and the souls of the people."[8]

Judaism has reached the goal; it is with God the Father. But it has paid a heavy price for the bliss of being with the Father. The staff of the synagogue is broken while the church is triumphant. Nevertheless, suffering is a small price to pay for the certainty that Israel is the eternal people; that nothing beyond its physical existence and the propagation of the holy seed of Abraham is necessary to assure the presence of God; that by its very existence Israel bears witness to God in the world.

Therefore Judaism has no need to engage in missionary activities; its sole task is to be, to go on living. The chapter on Judaism (entitled "The Fire, or: The Eternal Life") in his *Star of Redemption*, opens with the triumphant quotation from the prayerbook,

> "Blessed art Thou . . . . who hast planted eternal life in our midst." "The fire burns at the core of the star. The rays go forth only from this fire; then they radiate irresistibly to the outside. The fire of the core must burn incessantly. Its flame must eternally feed upon itself. It requires no fuel from

without. Time has no power over it and must roll past. It must produce its own time and reproduce itself forever. It must make its life everlasting in the succession of generations, each producing the generation to come and bearing witness to those gone by. It bears witness by bearing children — two meanings but one act in which eternal life is realized. Elsewhere, past and future are divorced, the one sinking back, the other coming on; here they grow into one. To bear the future is, at the same time, to bear witness to the past. The son is born so that he may bear witness to the father's father. The grandson renews the name of the forebear. The patriarchs of old call upon their last descendant by his name — which is theirs. Above the darkness of the future burns the star-strewn heaven of the promise: 'So shall thy seed be.' (Genesis 15.5)"

Here is what Rosenzweig considers to be the decisive difference between Judaism and Christianity as well as between Israel and all other nations. Israel "bears witness" to God by "bearing children," by the very fact of her biological existence and continuity. Christianity bears witness by its mission and numerical growth. Unlike all other nations, Israel has stepped outside history and the world; she is blind-folded insofar as her attention is fixed upon but one goal: redemption, the end of time and history, that moment beyond history when God will be One and His name, One; when Israel, too, will be redeemed from her separate existence. Prior to redemption, she is indifferent to history and wants but to survive until that moment.

Rosenzweig's strictly theological interpretations of Judaism is, of course, diametrically opposed to Jewish nationalism, the national interpretation of Jewish life and history offered by Zionism. Rosenzweig, as he once remarks, looks upon the work in Palestine with "repelled benevolence;" quoting Hermann Cohen, he can see in it only an "episode in modern Jewish history," another attempt to assure merely the physical survival of the Jewish people. Israel must forever struggle from the today to the tomorrow in order to survive and to have a "today." It is important that Israel survive, for any today may be the "today" of the Messiah; redemption must have its starting point in some "today," some point of existence in this world. In this sense, Rosenzweig approves of Zionism as he does of every effort designed to safeguard the physical security of the Jewish people and to vouchsafe its survival for that last moment. But he sharply rejects Zionism's definition of itself as the movement which has brought about the re-entry of the Jewish people into history. A people rooted in redemption and in "the end of time" cannot take part in the struggles unfolding within time. History is the concern of the *nations*. *They* struggle for their share and possessions in space and time, for they foresee and fear the time when they will no longer be and when their language will no longer be understood. "We Jews alone cannot imagine a time when we shall no longer be. For we have long ago been robbed of all the things in which the peoples of the world are rooted — land and language, custom and law. . . . Nevertheless, we are still living and will live forever. Our life is no longer interwoven with anything outside ourselves. We have no roots in the earth. Hence we are eternal wanderers, deeply rooted in our body and blood. And it is this rootedness in ourselves and in nothing but ourselves, that vouchsafes our eternity."[10]

Christianity, too, is eternal. Unaware of the Jewish origin of its task, it pursues its mission to the gentiles — the eternal rays radiating from the fire, pointing, like the beams of a cross, into all directions. The rays seek to penetrate the long night of time. God has withdrawn the Jew from the stream of time, building the bridge of the Law high above it. The Christian, however, challenges the stream of time; he struggles within history for the conversion of the gentiles. But that very stream of time is a sign to him that the end has not yet come. Thus Judaism is static eternity while Christianity is eternity within time. Christianity must forever change and grow while Judaism need but exist. The religious meaning of Jewish existence is to bear witness to redemption in a world as yet unredeemed, to anticipate redemption that still is to come to the others. The Jew cannot recognize Christianity's claim that it has *achieved* redemption: that it is the Messianic kingdom fulfilled; he can recognize, however, that the Christian world has overcome the pagan way of life and is *aiming* at redemption. Hence the Christian world, to the Jew, is redemption in process, and he recognizes it as a realm that mediates between a wholly unredeemed world and the kingdom of God.

This difference between Judaism and Christianity has profound implications for the individual. A Jew is born a Jew; a Christian requires baptism in order to overcome the pagan state of his birth. Hence the inner life of the Christian is more dynamic; the Jew is in greater danger of ossification. The Christian change of the day of rest from the Sabbath to Sunday symbolizes this distinction. The Sabbath is the festival of redemption. The Torah defines it as a memorial both of the work of creation and of the exodus from Egypt, of revelation. (Exodus 20.11; Deuteronomy 5.15.) The twin motives of creation and revelation are given expression in the Sabbath service. "On the eve of Sabbath, expression is given to the knowledge that the earth is a creation; in the morning [prayers], the people give utterance to their awareness of being elected through the gift of the Torah which signifies that eternal life has been planted in their midst."[11] But in the afternoon prayers of the Sabbath, "creation" and "revelation" point to "redemption" as the Sabbath wanes and the Jew prays for the day which will be the "complete Sabbath,"[12] the day of redemption for all peoples and thus the *end* of time.

Sunday, on the other hand, is the *beginning* of the week. The cross symbolizes the eternal task of beginning ever anew; the Christian is the eternal beginner. Hence, eternal *youth* is symbolic of the Christian while the *old* Jew is the symbol of Judaism. The Christian is a pagan at birth; the more Christian he becomes the farther away he moves from his origin. The Jew is born a Jew; the longer he lives the more he realizes his innate character. Hence the old Jew is the true image of the Jew.

So defined, Judaism and Christianity have irreducibly different yet organically related functions in the divine economy: "Israel: to represent, in time and history, the eternal kingdom of God, Christianity: to bring itself and the world toward that goal."[13] Their roads to the ultimate goal are different, but the goal itself is the same for both. Rosenzweig quotes with approval Yehuda Halevi, the great medieval thinker and poet of the Jewish exile, who compares Israel's relationship to her daughter religions with the relationship of the seed to the tree which sprang from the original seed but whose fruit now encapsules new seeds: "So it is concerning the religion of Moses. All later religions are transformed into it though externally they may reject it. They merely serve to introduce the expected Messiah and pave the way for him. He is the fruit, and all will be his fruit if they acknowledge him, and will become one tree. Then they will revere the root they formerly despised. . . . "[14]

IV

The traditional tension between Judaism and Christianity is harmoniously resolved by Rosenzweig: both are equally true in time. That his concept of Christianity is not in agreement with the dominant views of Jewish tradition has already been pointed out. But it is important to note that not even his Christian friends were prepared to agree with him.

Rosenstock rejected Rosenzweig's interpretation emphatically. How can Rosenzweig maintain that the spiritual continuity of Judaism is assured by the mere biological continuity of its adherents? The modern Jewish community is the product of racial admixture; different racial strains have entered into it, often through mixed marriages, even though the non-Jewish partner may have become converted to Judaism. It is absurd to speak of a "pure seed of Abraham" on which to base a metaphysical concept and interpretation of Judaism. The chosen people does no longer exist. Its role has been surrendered to Christianity, the new and universal Christian union of all men of good will, transcending all national limitations. It is not true that the Jews are still waiting for redemption. On the contrary. They have become so alienated, so far removed from their commitment to revelation that their actions deny the living reality of the word of God. "Judah claims that his chosenness is his divine right and implies no obligation; he is like Lucifer who, originally chosen by God, falls because he considers his chosenness only a divine title for privileges not a divine mandate for duties." In the same way, the Jew believes that God has bestowed inalienable and irrevocable rights upon him, rights which are his inalienably for no other reason than that they are hereditary. His success depends on the number of his children. Hence he loves life passionately, dies for no cause, no fatherland, no mission. But all this has come to an end. Rosenstock writes (November 19, 1916): "Do you think that the rise of Zionism is a coincidence? It is a logical development. Israel's time as the people of the Bible is past. The church has replaced the synagogue. The era of the Eternal Jew is ending, just as the Basques, Celts and other peoples have come to an end. For nations, too, have their eras. The place of the Eternal Jew is taken by another Zion. But this new Zion is something utterly different," a nation like all other nations, wholly different from the Zion of old.

Rosenstock feels that even the Old Testament has lost its role and meaning for the church. The church now has its own Old Testament, its own recorded history. It now has its own books of Judges, Kings and Prophets in its Councils, Popes and Church Fathers. Through Zionism, Judaism has once again entered history. Like every other young nation, it has re-entered the arena of the world in order to compete with other nations for a longer span of time. Therefore, it has abdicated its role in the divine scheme of redemption. The same is true of the Hebrew language: precisely because it may once more become a living language, rooted in the *physical* soil, the heritage of a living people, its *metaphysical* function can no longer be preserved.

Rosenstock's letter was written in 1916, one year before the Balfour Declaration. It was a sign of his perceptiveness that he took the Zionist movement seriously at a time when Zionism had hardly reached the colonizing stage, and that he saw Zionism's spiritual predicament and problems much more deeply than many Zionist thinkers themselves did. Only history will show whether Rosenzweig or Rosenstock is right. Neither of them, however, considered a third possibility: that Israel's new life in its own land might itself become a new expression of Jewish religious creativity. We shall consider this possibility in our discussion of Martin Buber and Aaron David Gordon.

V

Rosenzweig's Jewish development since his fateful discussions with Rosenstock was a gradual and patient appropriation of a Judaism which was still largely unknown to him. And precisely because he himself approached Judaism from the outside, as someone who had been a marginal Jew himself, he understood the problem of marginal Jews and continuously devised new methods of leading them toward Judaism. He taught Jewish courses in Kassel in the summer of 1920; then he moved to the larger community of Frankfort where he founded an entirely new type of Jewish educational institution, the *Freies Jüdisches Lehrhaus*. He himself defined it as a modern *Beth Ha-midrash*. Its task is to spread the knowledge of Judaism; but this task has to be performed in a new way. German Jews have a passion for "general culture"; hence Judaism will have to be presented as a part of general culture; it must be "smuggled in," as it were. The German Jew must be made ashamed of his ignorance of Jewish matters.

In 1917, Rosenzweig had already published a brochure, *It is Time*, in which he dealt with the problem of Jewish culture. The problem did not cease to engage his attention. As he saw it, Jewish culture must mean to the Jew not only more but something qualitatively different from what culture means to other nations and religions. For the Jew, "learning" is not the mere acquisition of knowledge; learning "begins where the subject matter ceases to be subject matter and is transformed into inner power."[15] As the Jew "learns," he himself becomes a link in the chain of tradition and the subject of study for future generations, he has increased the substance of tradition even though he may have added only the most modest insight, interpretation, or idea. In Judaism, study is the process of perpetual self-renewal.

Though no educator himself, Rosenzweig was so deeply convinced of the crucial role of Jewish education that he ventured to outline a curriculum for Jewish religious schools. His primary aim was to lead the student back to the sources. The same concern motivated another recommendation: His proposal to establish an *Akademie für die Wissenschaft des Judentums*. He envisioned not only an academy devoted to research and scholarship but also a center for the spiritual and intellectual regeneration of Jewish educators in Germany. Every teacher was to be a scholar and every scholar, a teacher. Hermann Cohen took up Rosenzweig's proposal and publicly called for its realization.[16] The research division of the *Akademie* was established but Rosenzweig's hopes for its educational division remained unfulfilled even though he considered it of greater importance since the adequate training of Jewish teachers alone could vouchsafe the continuity of Judaism.

Rosenzweig had concluded the *Star of Redemption* with the words: *Into Life!* This phrase gradually became the keyword of all his Jewish activities. He asked: What must we *do* in order to go into life? How must we live as Jews so that our Jewishness will be embodied in our acts? His answer was two-fold: Learning and the Law. In 1917, he had already outlined his concept of Jewish "learning" in *It is Time*; but the "Law" as the embodiment of Jewish life played an equally dominant role in his *Letters* and thinking, and in 1923 he published *The Builders*, an epistle addressed to Martin Buber, in which he dealt with the place of Law, its study and practice, in Judaism.[17]

His concept of Jewish Law is a synthesis of the positions of orthodoxy and liberalism, affirming both yet transcending them at the same time. On the one hand, the Law is an objective reality imposed upon the individual; it is "the law of the millennia, studied and lived, analyzed and rhapsodized, the Law of every day and of the day of death, petty and yet sublime, sober and yet woven into legend; a law which knows both the fire of the Sabbath candle and of the martyr's stake."[18] On the other hand, the individual must retain the right of choice. Orthodoxy is wrong in trying to freeze the living reality of the law in fixed paragraphs, in legal codes such as the *Shulḥan Arukh*. The law is essentially a process, and we, the Jews of today, are responsible participants in this process. No one can tell us in advance, prior to the moment when we ourselves practice the law, what is still alive for us and what may no longer be relevant to us. The law is of today and not of yesterday; open, not closed; developing and changing, not changeless and completed. It was certainly regarded as something contemporaneous, open and living by the rabbis of the Talmud who created a large portion of the traditional law and under whose ministrations the law developed. The law is not something unalterable, completed in the past; every new generation has the task to re-create it for itself. Our task is to live up to the daring word of Deuteronomy: "The Lord made this covenant not with our fathers but with us, even us who are all of us here alive this day." (Deuteronomy 5.3).

Orthodoxy claims the right and capacity to determine the objectively valid boundaries of the law, to define the precise distinction between the allowed and the forbidden. Rosenzweig vigorously maintains that "we do not know the boundary." An act which is permitted by orthodoxy may appear prohibited to the religious sensitivity of the modern Jew. The religious consciousness of the modern Jew may discover new *mitzvot*, new commandments and prohibitions. "We do not know how far the pegs of the tent of the Torah may be moved outward nor which of our actions are destined to move them."

Rosenzweig recognized Judaism as a religion of law in principle, but reserved the right of personal decision.

He unconditionally rejected the alternative of "all or nothing." He accepted no *Shulḥan Arukh a priori*, no "table which someone else has prepared" for him. He observed *kashruth* in his own home, for instance, but was prepared to eat non-kosher food outside his home. "We want a home, not a ghetto. Every Jew should be able to eat in our home; but we also want to be able to visit the Christian who invites us to eat with him. Our Jewishness is not a matter of eating and drinking."

Rosenzweig did not observe all *mitzvot*; he made a selection from among them. In this respect, his position is close to the approach of liberal Judaism to the problem of observance. However, he also emphasized the distinctions between his approach and that of liberal Judaism. He did not want his own approach to become the basis of a Reform *Shulḥan Arukh*. "We leave Judaism the way it is; we do not intend to reform it. Judaism will continue to reform itself, just as it has always done in the past. We do not intend to erect a new house beside or in the place of the old house of orthodoxy. We simply endeavor to erect tents, with the full knowledge that they are tents and not a house, because at the place where we happen to be there is no house. But we must have a roof over our heads. Should we find a house we shall gladly enter it. For us, observance of the law precedes its theoretical justification. In liberal Judaism the reverse is the case."[19] He rejected the claim that Judaism was "identical with the law; Judaism is not identical with the law; it creates it. Judaism itself is not law;

Judaism is: to be a Jew." The practice of the *mitzvot* is prior to any theorizing about their meaning.

Rosenzweig aligned himself with liberal Judaism when he stressed that Jewish law did not represent a rigid, unchangeable code but was the product of an evolutionary process. However, he accepted the principle that law has a vital function in Judaism. He knew that his own position was at best provisional, but he was certain that it would lead to some form of observance. When someone once asked him whether he laid *tefillin* during the morning prayers, he answered, significantly, "not yet." He did not underestimate the difficulties of principle and practice inherent in his position. In one of his letters,[20] he discussed his attitude toward the Sabbath and its observance. "Initially and as a matter of principle, I refrained merely from writing business letters on the Sabbath but not from letters for private enjoyment. However, I had to stop this liberal kind of Sabbath observance when Rothschild, during a discussion of a *Lehrhaus* problem, expected me to write something down since I 'was writing anyhow on the Shabbat.' Only then did I realize that such subtle distinctions could not be made unless everyone made them, and it was this experience which drove me, albeit with a heavy heart, to follow the orthodox practice."

Nevertheless, Rosenzweig was hopeful that a new law would gradually emerge. "After the completion of the Talmud, there has been a highway common to all Jews. To be sure, there were side roads, bridges, towns; but essentially there was only one main road.

For the past one hundred and fifty years, that common highway has no longer been in existence. Its extension [modern orthodoxy] is at best one of many roads; it is no longer *the* way. The only unity we possess today is the countryside through which we travel. Some day, a main highway may again lead through it. I believe this will happen again though I anticipate that we shall have not just one road but a system of roads. The time for such a system has not yet come; but our individual roads are the proper preparation for it."[21]

The laws which can be observed are not arbitrarily chosen. Their observance emerges from an inner "must," a compelling inner affirmation of their meaning and validity. This inner "must" does not arise by itself. Man must probe and search for it. We *must* do whatever we *can*, and one day we may discover that we *can* do what we *must*; by doing what we can we shall ultimately no longer be able to do without. In this way we can appropriate the law; it will be *ours* as a natural religious possession of our own.

The notion of the transformation of the "can" into the living reality of the "must" is the decisive difference between Rosenzweig's position and that of liberal Judaism. Yehuda Halevi made a similar distinction in his *Kusari* when he pointed out the dangers which arise from the assertion that it is permissible to make selections from the law: If a man is permitted to make his own selections from the law because he feels he cannot obey a law which his reason cannot comprehend even though it may be divinely revealed, then "each man may choose whatever form of belief may enter his speculation."[22] Freedom of choice may open the gate to anarchy; this is the strongest argument in favor of orthodoxy. But Rosenzweig exorcised this danger by making the choice between the laws which a Jew "can" or "cannot" fulfill not a matter of caprice, taste or personal preference, but of a man's ultimate and most earnest seriousness. He knew that his road might conceivably lead to anarchy — for what one man "can" and even "must" do, another cannot. What mattered to Rosenzweig was not that all Jews arrive at the same "must" as far as the law is concerned, but that their decision should grow out of a deep sense of responsibility and not be motivated by indifference, intellectual laziness or frivolity.

In his quest for a "new law" Rosenzweig differed, in principle, also from the position of traditional Judaism although in practice he lived by its laws. His approach was revolutionary. Convinced that the modern Jew must not only be heir to the past but also creator of the future, he initiated a discussion of the law which continues to agitate the best Jewish minds — a discussion to be continued less with words than with deeds and ways of life.

Rosenzweig headed the school which he had founded for only two years. In January 1922 he was stricken by a disease which confined him to his bed for seven years. In December 1922, his fingers became paralyzed and he lost his capacity for writing. For a time he still was able to dictate. In May 1923 he lost the use of his voice and could communicate only by using a specially constructed typewriter. When his muscles grew too weak for its use, he struggled to give signals with almost unperceptible movements of one finger which his wife attempted to sense and write down. In these years of extreme suffering Rosenzweig produced a German translation and luminous commentary to the poems of Yehuda Halevi and began a translation of the Bible in cooperation with Martin Buber. His life ebbed away on December 10, 1929. His last seven years of suffering were sanctified by his heroism. It was the heroism of the Jew — of the servant of God.

CHAPTER FOUR

MARTIN BUBER: LIFE AS DIALOGUE

There are many ways of approaching God and of serving Him. Rosenzweig turned to faith while yet a young man. After a brief period of preoccupation with philosophical idealism, he realized that his primary problem was not to believe but what to believe; not whether to choose faith but what faith to choose. Above all, he sought an answer to the question whether, in his day, there still was a uniquely Jewish way to God.

Martin Buber, one of Rosenzweig's closest friends and collaborators during the last years of the latter's life, had to travel a much longer and more complicated road to faith.

Born in Vienna in 1878, Buber lived in an atmosphere of religious and scholarly "enlightenment" at his grandfather's home in Lemberg, Galicia, until he was fourteen. There he had his first contact with Hasidism which was to become one of the decisive influences in his life and thought.

Buber began his public career as a German writer and spokesman for Zionism at the turn of the century. He had joined the emerging Zionist movement while he was still a student, and in 1901 became the editor of the Zionist periodical, *Die Welt*. He was closely identified with cultural Zionism, that wing of the movement which, under the influence of Aḥad Ha-am, opposed the purely political program represented by Herzl and Nordau. It envisioned the renaissance of Jewish culture rather than the political rebirth of the Jewish people as the ultimate goal of the Zionist movement. Buber felt that nationality could not be an end in itself; at the same time he was convinced that a man's nationality was the sole means by which a person or people could become creative.[1] A Jew could contribute to the general culture and welfare of the world only as a member of the Jewish nation. For this reason, the vitality and creativity of the Jewish spirit could be renewed only through the return of a substantial number of Jews to their homeland.

However, neither Herzl's political Zionism, nor Aḥad Ha-am's cultural Zionism had associated the national rebirth of the Jewish people with a return to faith. The early programs calling for a renewal of Jewish national existence and creativity did not include a call for the renewal of loyalty to the religious forms and values of the Jewish tradition. In fact, the Hebrew and Yiddish writers who were the chief spokesman and interpreters of the Zionist idea in Eastern Europe during the last decades of the 19th century, had developed their themes in radical opposition to the religious traditionalism which still dominated their communities. The writings of men such as Micah Joseph Berdichevski, Saul Tchernichovsky, Judah Leib Gordon, and even of the young Bialik reflected a strong anti-religious sentiment. Buber, too, considered Zionism merely the instrument for the national and cultural but not for the religious rebirth of the Jewish people. A long development toward faith lay still ahead.

Buber was aware of and alive to the intellectual tendencies of his day. The vast shifts taking place in European philosophical thought all had their impact on him, yet the decisive influence in his development was Hasidism.

Shortly after Herzl's death in 1904, Buber withdrew completely from Zionist activities and devoted several years to an intensive study of the Hasidic sources. Though the last great religious movement in Judaism until our time, Hasidism was hardly known or, if known, generally regarded with contempt by Western Jewry and the *Maskilim*, the spokesmen of "enlightenment" of the east. For example, Graetz' discussion of Hasidism in his *History of the Jews* was written with a pen dipped in scorn, without the slightest attempt to understand or appreciate it. And many of the writers of the East regarded it as a superstition standing in the path of progress.

Buber's readings of Hasidic texts and especially some sayings of the *Besht*, the founder of Hasidism, about the daily inward renewal of the pious man, gradually strengthened Buber's feeling that the essence of Judaism could be found in *ḥasidut*, personal piety.[2] After years of painstaking efforts, Buber succeeded in freeing the image of Hasidism from the distortions engendered by misunderstanding and hostility and his books introduced it to the thought and literature of the Western world.[3]

His approach to the subject was not that of the objective scholar who analyzes and presents his facts with complete detachment. He was engaged in a continuous dialogue with the Hasidic masters and leaders about whom he was writing. In speaking of them, he discovered that they were speaking to him and that they represented what he felt was the essence of the Jewish character in modern times.

I

The Hasidism of the eighteenth century had taken over an important doctrine from the Kabbalists of the sixteenth century: throughout the world, sparks of the *shekhinah*, of the divine presence, can be found. We encounter God in all phases and aspects of life. God can be seen in everything, in people and things, in organic and in inorganic nature, for nothing exists without a divine spark. Though these sparks are imprisoned in shells of darkness (the *kelipot*) and weighed down by impurity and profaneness, no sphere of reality is devoid of them. They are waiting to be released from their shells so that they can return to their divine essence.

It is man who can liberate them through the act of *teshuvah*, turning and returning to God. Man is literally God's partner, His co-worker in the never-ending work of creation, for his action releases the divine in the world and lifts it to ever greater perfection. Thus religious life finds its consummation in the union of *experience* and *act*: man's knowledge of God is confirmed through dedicated action. Therefore, there can be no division between religion and ethics. Man's relation to God becomes embodied in his relations to his fellow-men. In his acts, every individual discharges the responsibility for that segment of the world that is entrusted to him.[4]

These Hasidic notions had a profound influence on the development of Buber's thought and are a key to the understanding of his philosophy. It is possible to enter into a living relationship with all things. Each man whom I meet, each object which I encounter, waits for me to enter into a relationship with it. Everything turns into a "living" reality through the discovery of the divine spark in it. In Buber's words, "real life is meeting."[5] All life is encounter.

II

Buber makes a radical distinction between the two basic attitudes of which men are capable, the two fundamental situations into which they enter. He describes them by what he calls the "primary words" *I-Thou* and *I-It*. The emphasis here is not on the components but on their relationship. The primary word *I-Thou* designates a relation of person to person, of subject to subject, a relation of reciprocity and mutuality involving meeting or encounter. The primary word *I-It* designates the connection of individual to thing, of subject to object, involving some form of utilization, domination or control. Even so-called objective knowledge involves an *I-It* relationship. On the other hand, the *I-Thou* situation is relation *par excellence*, for it is through this relation, into which man can enter only with the whole of his being, that the person in his authentic personality emerges: Through the Thou who stands over against him a man becomes an I.[6]

To follow Buber in his full application of this idea involves a radical departure from our customary mode of thinking. We find little difficulty in speaking of another person as "Thou." We address him; we listen to him as he speaks to us. There is a relationship of reciprocity and mutuality. However, we are certain that things do not "speak" in the same way. A poet may look at a moss-grown rock and describe the sense of cosmic awe and infinity the rock conveys to him. But he does not claim that the rock "speaks" to him. He projects his personal feelings into the rock; he bestows his personal emotions upon it. He does not describe what the rock "says." He describes his personal feelings in the presence of the rock. There is no real mutuality. The world — in this case, the rock — is an object of experience, but it is wholly passive, indifferent to the fact that it is being experienced.

In the *I-Thou* relationship, however, there is no passivity. Buber maintains that there is a mutuality both with animate and inanimate nature, yea, even with what he calls "spiritual beings." "The spheres in which the world of relation is built are three. First, our life with nature, in which relation clings to the threshold of speech. Second, our life with men, in which the relation takes on the form of speech. Third, our life with spiritual beings, where the relation, being without speech, yet begets it."[7] Everything, from ideal essences to a seemingly trivial thing can "address" man. It can "speak" to him, signify a meaning, be a source of revelation. It becomes a "Thou," that which is not merely passively perceived but actively enters into the perceiving.

He who approaches a thing in readiness will be encountered by it as a living "Thou." Buber tells of an experience he once had when, as a boy of eleven, he spent a summer on the farm of his grandparents.

> "As often as I could do it unobserved, I used to steal into the stable and gently stroke the neck of my favorite, a broad dapple-grey horse. It was not a casual delight but a great, certainly friendly, yet also deeply stirring happening. . . . When I stroked the mighty mane . . . . and felt the life beneath my hand, it was as though the element of vitality itself bordered on my skin — something that was not I, was certainly not akin to me, palpably the other, not just another, really the Other itself; and yet it let me approach, confided itself to me, placed itself elementally in the relation of *Thou* and *Thou* with me. The horse, even when I had not begun by pouring oats for him into the manger, very gently raised his massive head, ears twitching, then snorted quietly, as a conspirator gives a signal meant to be recognizable only by his fellow-conspirator; and I was approved."[8]

But such moments come to an end; the I-Thou relationship between man and animal, hardly established, breaks up; the Thou becomes an It. What had been a genuine relationship has become a mere "experience." What at one moment is the Thou of an I-Thou relationship, becomes an It in the next.

This alternation in our situations is a universal human experience and affects what happens between men in every aspect of their lives. For example, as Victor von Weizsäcker has said, ideally, a physician ought to be "sick with the sickness of the patient." He ought to take on the sickness of the patient as a personal task, treating the whole person, not merely symptom and causes. He should deal with the patient as a person, not merely as a case; and he himself ought to respond to the patient as a person and not simply as a practitioner of medical skills.[9]

Unfortunately, a busy physician rarely retains sufficient time or the inner reserves to enter into this kind of relationship with every patient. Hence the patient becomes — or remains — a case, an It.

A social worker is similarly entrusted with the care of a human being in need. He experiences the Thou in this person: their trust and interaction are mutual even though the difference in function between him who cares and him who is cared for persists. However, as the case load of the social worker increases, the power of relationship decreases. Once again, the "person" becomes a "case" and the Thou degenerates into an It. A routine born of experience takes the place of a genuine "relationship." Every new case remains an It that does not become a Thou. To deal with persons as "cases" has advantages: less time, effort, and involvement are required if one can use a technique or system of dealing with a person's symptoms rather than with the person himself. A heavy workload can be handled more smoothly and efficiently. The system may be excellent; nevertheless, it destroys the possibility of a genuine mutual relationship. The Thou has become an It. Buber feels that there are social workers whose lives are completely dedicated to their work yet who know only "clients" and "cases" and who have not spoken even once to a fellowman as a Thou.

Buber uses the term "dialogical" to describe the *I-Thou* relationship, and some of his most significant essays are published under the title *Dialogisches Leben* (Dialogical Life).[10] This volume deals with educational as well as with philosophical issues, for Buber considers the relationship between teacher and student as a particularly clear example of that mutuality which must be an integral part of every genuine relationship. The teacher's task is to educate his pupils; however, if he is an authentic teacher, he is as much educated by them as they are by him. Another area in which this dialogic relation is seen at work, that of psychiatry, is described by Buber in the lectures he delivered at the Washington School of Psychiatry.[11]

The dialogue between man and man is the fundamental fact of human existence. It is in dialogue — whether silent or spoken — between the I and the Thou that man's personality actually comes into being.

Buber thus firmly rejects the social theories of both individualism and collectivism. Individualism errs in assuming that the individual is or can be the primary datum of human existence: society does not result from the simple addition of unrelated, isolated individuals. Collectivism errs because the individual is not simply an abstraction from a collectivity. A collectivistic society does not truly liberate the individual from his isolation when it offers him the spurious security of being part of the mass; it merely depersonalizes him and deprives him of his individuality.

The fundamental datum of human existence is neither the individual nor the group but the relationship of one man to another or to others. "In the beginning is relation." All real life is dialogue, meeting.

III

This concept is fundamental to Buber's philosophical anthropology, his understanding of man. It is, at the same time, the key to his theology. The relationship of man to man is for Buber the analogy of the divine-human relationship, except for one crucial difference.

We have seen that every Thou is doomed to recede into an It because we lack the power of relation. Even the relationship of love does not last in its immediacy; often it is latent but not present; it alternates between potentiality and actuality. Mutuality breaks off; the Thou escapes us and becomes depersonalized; it is transformed into a neutral object, an It.

However, there is one Thou that by its very nature remains Thou to us and never becomes an It. This Thou, in Buber's language, is the Eternal Thou, God. Every man who calls God encounters this Thou regardless of the name by which he may address Him. The Eternal Thou is met even by the man who does not believe in God, yet "gives his whole being to addressing the Thou of his life, as a Thou," as something that commands his unconditional loyalty, an absolute "that cannot be limited by another."[12] This man, too, addresses God.

Yet how can we be certain that there is such a Thou that can be addressed and is eternally present? Is it not an integral part of human existence to experience the absence of God? From Biblical times on, men of faith have cried out in anguish that God has hidden His face. Prophets and psalmists who knew God also knew the bitter experience of being separated from God, of being alone in the anguish of an empty heart.

For Buber, this experience can and does occur, but it is falsely interpreted. God never hides His face; He is never other than Thou to us; He is always present. It is we who are not always present and who do not open the channels leading from God to us. To support this view, Buber draws on a new interpretation of the passage in Exodus, "*Eheyeh asher Eheyeh*," usually translated as "I am that I am." Buber translates the passage differently: "I shall be present as I shall be present."[13] God is present in every now and here. The man who has a preconceived notion of how God is present as a Thou will fail to recognize or acknowledge God's presence. We hide our faces from God by limiting the mode, manner, place and time of God's presence.

For Buber, God is present in every relationship, in all dialogue, and speaks through it to us. We are met by God not in the extra-ordinary event, the unusual moment, the so-called mystical experience but, as Hasidism had shown him, in the ordinariness of everyday life. Every moment, every day, every thing and event which may appear trivial to the superficial observer, has the capacity of becoming the mediator of the Eternal Thou. In a particularly tragic passage in his essay, "Dialogue," Buber tells of the "conversion" he underwent from his previous emphasis on the religious character of the "exceptional" to his recognition of the religious character of the ordinary. He writes of an occasion when he was so full of "religious enthusiasm" that he failed to recognize the question that was being put to him in and by the life of another person. His failure made him realize that the encounter with God is not something apart from but involved in every day life. "Since then I have given up the 'religious' which is nothing but the exception, extraction, exaltation, ecstacy . . . . I possess nothing but the everyday out of which I am never taken." This is, of course, the Hasidic notion that the relation to anything can be lifted up to a point where it becomes a relation to the divine.

We speak and are spoken to. However, the revelation of God to man, the divine-human encounter, is not a supernatural event. "The signs bearing the word are nothing outside the ordinary . . . ., but simply what happens by way of normal occurrence." They are, of course, signs only if they are understood as they want to be understood. Thus the world is continually filled with the possibility of revelation — revelation which, for Buber, is man's encounter with God's presence rather than information about His essence.

IV

It is here that we are directed to one of the most Jewish aspects of Buber's conception of God. For Buber, the characteristic feature of the Biblical concept of God is that *He may be spoken to.* In his book, *Moses*,[14] he observes that "the soul of the Decalogue . . . . is to be found in the word 'Thou' " with which God addresses every individual. God reveals Himself as Thou; more precisely, it is this Thou that reveals Him. However, the relationship between God and man in which God addresses man as Thou does not require that the individual to whom God speaks be in a state of isolation or loneliness, that he be withdrawn from the world, negate or reject it, as Kierkegaard taught. Buber insists that it is wrong to negate the world in order to reach God. The world is not an illusion; nor could a God who can be reached by us only if we were to break off all relations to the world, be the God of the *whole* world. For Buber, the world itself may become a revelation of God; finite Thou, it discloses the Eternal Thou who speaks through it.

Thus it is in community that God is most truly revealed and realized. Community is not a mechanical association of isolated self-seeking individuals; true community, as opposed to mere collectivity, is the place in which the divine is realized in the living relations of men. The establishment of this kind of community is, for Buber, the central demand and challenge of Judaism. "The yearning of Judaism for God is the yearning to prepare a resting place for Him in genuine community. Judaism's understanding of Israel is the understanding that from that people genuine community is to spring. Its Messianic expectation is the expectation of genuine community fully realized." God must not remain an abstract concept. He is confirmed by the community that is a "holy community." He is confirmed by every society that bears witness to Him and strives to be the bearer of the kingdom of God.

In the same way, the individual can actualize his inward experience of the presence of God in all of his personal actions. The demand of God upon us confronts us in every aspect of our every-day life. In the dialogue between God and man, "God speaks to each man through the life He has given him and in which He upholds him. And the only way in which man responds to Him is with his whole life — in the way he lives it." The Jewish teaching of the unity and oneness of God corresponds to its teaching of the oneness and all-inclusiveness of life. God gives man not merely spirit but existence in all its parts, from the lowest to the highest. Man's partnership with God cannot be confined or reduced to mere "spiritual" attitudes, to devout feelings or a superstructure of ritual practices. It requires his whole life, in all its aspects and relationships. Man can have no real part in holiness without the sanctification of his every-day life.

The history of Judaism discloses that it has always opposed so-called "religion" because it has seen in it the attempt to buy off God, who demands all, with a limited segment of life. Thus Hasidism which for Buber is the consummation of Judaism in the Diaspora, no longer maintains any distinction between sacred and secular, between holy and profane. The common event has itself become a sacrament. Hasidism does not recognize the profane as a realm of reality in its own right. "Profane" merely designates that which is not yet sanctified. "The physical, the animal, the creaturely are waiting to be sanctified. The self-same passion that results in evil can, when turned toward God, bring forth the good. There are not two realms, that of spirit and not of nature; there is only the coming kingdom of God."

V

In our discussion of Rosenzweig we saw Judaism and Christianity conceived as two religious systems which possess an equal claim to truth. Buber disagrees with Rosenzweig. He rejects any suggestion that the redemption might already be an accomplished fact.

"The Jew *feels* unredeemedness physically and in his flesh. He carries the burden of an unredeemed world. He *cannot* concede that redemption is an accomplished fact, for he knows that it is not so. We know of no redeemer who has appeared at one point in history in order to inaugurate a new and redeemed history. Nothing which has already happened can give us rest; hence we are directed with all our being toward that which is yet to come."

Buber, then, rejects the doctrine most essential to Christianity. He stated his views in an address to a conference of Christian missionary societies in 1930. However, his position toward Christianity would be incompletely recorded without the remarks with which he concluded his address:[15]

> "What then do we both have in common? To put it in the most concrete manner: a book and an expectation. For you, the book is only the antechamber, for us it is the sanctuary itself. Nevertheless, it is the same place, and in it we may listen together to the voice which speaks in it. That is to say, we can labor together digging for the speech which is buried, liberating the living word which is imprisoned. Your expectation is for the second coming, ours for a coming of what has not yet been. Nevertheless, we can wait together for that one thing which is to come; and there are moments in which we may pave the road for it in joint effort. Our fortunes are divorced from each other in the pre-Messianic era. Here the Jew is incomprehensible to the Christian; he is the stiffnecked one who refuses to see what has happened. The Christian is equally incomprehensible to the Jew; he is the presumptuous

one who asserts redemption as an accomplished fact in a world which is unredeemed. This schism no human power can bridge. But it does not preclude harmonious cooperation in watching for the oneness coming from God. For all the truths of faith held by men this oneness will substitute the truth of the reality of God. And that truth is one. If we, both Christians and Jews, are really and truly concerned with God rather than with our own concepts of Him, then we are united in the vision that the house of our Father is different from the concepts formed by our all-too-human thinking."

CHAPTER FIVE

A. D. GORDON: THE RECOVERY OF COSMIC UNITY

In March 1920, a significant Jewish meeting took place in Prague: A conference of the Hapoel Hazair and the Zeire Zion. Hapoel Hazair represented the Zionist youth movement of Germany and Palestine, Zeire Zion was the Zionist youth movement of Polish Jewry. The conference had been called to stimulate and facilitate the immigration of *ḥalutzim* into Palestine and to formulate an ideological platform for the *ḥalutz* movement. The Central European group was headed by Buber, the Palestinian by Aaron David Gordon, then a man of 64 — an old man among the young people. "What is happening here," he said at the conference, "is not that we speak to you; it is our land that speaks to you. We are here merely to express what the land itself is saying. We say to you, to our entire people: *the land is waiting for you.*"

Buber and Gordon, the two leaders of the conference, shared the conviction that the return of the people of Israel to Palestine had a profound religious significance and that Israel's return to its land would accomplish its ultimate purpose only by the realization of its religious meaning. "Realization" became the key word of the pioneers of the labor movement, and Gordon was the outstanding religious personality to emerge from the Jewish labor movement of Palestine.

Gordon's family came from Vilna. His father, Uri, was a deeply religious person and a strictly observant Jew but free from fanaticism and dogmatism. He moved to Podolia where Aaron David was born in 1856. The boy was frail and required constant medical attention. He spent his youth on a farm in order to build up his physical strength. A private teacher was employed for his Jewish education. Later, he taught himself European languages and science with the knowledge and approval of his parents. Aaron David was thus spared the conflict which was typical for the young Russian Jew of his generation who as a rule could satisfy his desire for European learning only in rebellion against his parents. His years in the village were one of his significant formative periods. The ties which bound him to farm and forest are a key to his philosophy.

In 1880, Baron Horace Günzburg, a distant relative, appointed Gordon to an administrative post at one of his estates in Mohynia. Gordon remained at this post for twenty-three years. He appreciated the fact that his job provided a measure of security; nevertheless, he considered it a burden. Office work was alien to his nature. His deepest concerns and interests lay elsewhere. When his two children were ready to enter school, he began to concern himself with the educational problems of the local community. He invited young people to evenings of readings, discussions and music at his home, delivered lectures at the local synagogue on Sabbath afternoons, founded a library, and stimulated the planning and development of modernized schools for the community. When his daughter was old enough to begin her Hebrew studies, he founded a Hebrew school for girls.

Gordon's extraordinary pedagogic talents became one of the main reasons for his tremendous influence upon the labor movement. He was a gifted teacher but rejected a career as a professional educator for the same reason for which his grandfather had refused to accept a rabbinical post. His grandfather, a well-known talmudic scholar, had not wanted to make the teaching of the Torah the source of his livelihood; the grandson did not want to commercialize his interest in education. He did not even want to derive material benefits from his literary efforts and invariably returned the honoraria which he received for articles and essays that had been accepted for publication.

I

Gordon was forty-seven years old when he began to explore the possibility of going to Palestine as a common laborer. The plan involved a radical change in his life and that of his family. Palestine attracted him. His inner voice told him to go. But what was to become of his family? As a common laborer in Palestine he would be unable to support his wife, at least initially. Did he have the moral right to follow his conscience? Could he disregard the feelings of his parents who did not want to lose their son? For months Gordon lived in an agony of indecision. Then his parents passed away unexpectedly, one shortly after the other. Their passing ended his hesitation. His two children were grown up; he felt his wife could remain with them in Russia until he would have established himself in Palestine. He took the decisive step and left for Palestine in the spring of 1904.

Gordon had never done physical labor and was untrained, aging, and in poor health. Moreover, the Jewish laborer in Palestine faced great difficulties at that time. Like the German and Swedish settlers before them, the early Jewish settlers used Arab labor exclusively. The employment of Jewish labor was a new concept which had first been advanced by the immigrants of the Second *Aliyah* who had been influenced by the ideology of Russian socialism. Their demand not to use Arab but Jewish farm hands required a complete reorientation on the part of the Jewish settlers. The Jewish farm hand was physically untrained and therefore inferior to the Arab as a laborer; yet he had a higher standard of living and therefore commanded higher wages.

At first, Gordon, by now a man of nearly 50 and an intellectual, was unable to find employment on a Jewish farm. People had no faith in his physical resiliency. Someone offered him an administrative post but Gordon turned it down. Finally he found work in an orange grove. Happily he wrote to his family, "I feel like a child newborn. The labor tires the body, but it gives so much to the soul." A few months later, he found another job involving night work in the wine cellars of Rishon l'Zion. He earned little and had to share his room with seven people. Nevertheless he managed to save some money and was able to send small sums to his wife from time to time. His life in those years was the life of all Jewish laborers: periods of work alternating with periods of unemployment, interrupted by months of malaria. Unemployment or health insurance were still unknown. Mutual assistance alone tided people over periods of illness or unemployment. In 1908, Gordon was able to send for his daughter. She reported about the moment of their reunion: "When he came aboard to welcome me I was shocked by the great change in his appearance. He had become an old man; his hair was white, his clothes were shabby. But his expression and his shining eyes made me forget this first impression immediately."[1]

Gordon's wife arrived in Palestine in 1909 and the reunited family settled in Ein Ganim near Petach Tikva. Gordon was a unique figure among the members of the settlement. Most of them had left their families and Europe as young men in order to go to Palestine as pioneers. A generation older than most others, Gordon became their father, friend and teacher. One of his fellow workers reported an incident which shows the extraordinary impact of his personality and singular pedagogic talent: "Once we sat in a small room in a tight circle around Gordon. We discussed the despair which had gripped most of us, the disappointments we had to face continuously, and the flight from the country on the part of the disillusioned. We asked whether a Jewish laborer could have a family life and discussed a number of similar questions. Gordon listened carefully both to those who voiced their bitterness and despair as well as to those who opposed defeatism and countered it with a "nevertheless." However, even in the words of those who spoke hopefully of the future, one could discern a sense of stubborn determination rather than a quiet confidence or intellectual clarity about the ultimate goal of our life in Palestine. Gordon listened to everything, softly humming a melody. Suddenly he entered the conversation. And with his very first words he touched a chord in us, a chord of profound confidence in ourselves. A new spirit began to pervade our group. He gave us courage and strength and eased the burden of our hearts."[2]

II

Gordon's world view is rooted in the conviction that the cosmos has unity, that nature and man are one, and that all men are but organic parts of the cosmos. The term "cosmic" represents the central category of his thinking. It designates the basic point of view from which he illuminates all problems, be they political issues, the position of women in the modern world, the Jewish attitude toward the Arabs, or religious problems.

What is man's position in the cosmos? Man — and man alone of all beings known to us — is molded and influenced by the cosmos in two different ways: through his consciousness and knowledge of the world; and through his intuitive apperception of the world, much of which can never be consciously known, yet can be lived and experienced. What we *know* is merely a fragment of what we *are*. The individuality of a person does not manifest itself in his knowledge of reality which he derives from his senses and intellect; a man becomes an individual by the way he opens himself to the immediacy of the experience of life. For Gordon the human soul is related to a hidden part of the cosmos, to a life which remains hidden because, though we live and experience it, we cannot consciously know it. It is in this "hidden" life that each man's individuality is rooted. The deeper a man sinks his roots into this hidden part of the cosmos, the more significant will his grasp and understanding of life be.

Gordon is conscious of the fact that his theory sets up a dichotomy between rational "knowledge" and "life." He compares their dualism with the relationship between the flame and the oil in a burning lamp. Consciousness and knowledge are the flame, life itself is the oil which nourishes it. He also employs an analogy with an optic lens to explain his approach. Just as an optic lens concentrates light upon one point and leaves everything else in darkness, the intellect achieves clarity by concentrating its light on a single sector of reality. However, the intellect pays a price for this clarity: It cuts off the living relationship between the sector which it investigates and the totality of the cosmos. The more a man penetrates nature with his *knowledge*, the less he can *live* and *experience* it with his whole being. Yet the ultimate source of our deepest certainties is not the knowledge we may accumulate but life itself. We are certain of our own existence because of the immediacy of our experience of life itself. Reason can never achieve this certainty; it is pre-rational. The deepest essence of life cannot be grasped by the intellect or "proved" by reason or scientific method. It is life itself which makes our intellect and its knowledge possible. We are not because we think; we think because we are. Living intuition speaks where our intellect fails us.

Thus, man possesses two organs of perception: immediate intuition, and conscious comprehension (cognition) by the intellect. Man's possession of these two organs differentiates him from all other beings known to him. The intellect is an asset; it is an important weapon in the struggle for survival. At the same time, however, it tends to isolate and alienate man from the cosmos as a whole.

In the distant past, man and nature were one. Man had not yet emerged as a separate entity. He could not be distinguished from other creatures in nature, just as a swimmer cannot see his reflection unless he raises his head above the surface of the water. Man's state was altered radically when he raised his head above the "water" and *human thinking* came into being. Since that time, a cleavage has separated man's soul from all other creatures. He not only *is*; he *knows* that he is. His capacity to think is rooted in his alienation from nature; his alienation from nature is rooted in his capacity to think. For this reason man simultaneously has a sense of power and of impotence. He feels he has greatness: he can dominate nature and control it. At the same time, he is lonely and isolated in the cosmos and therefore afraid. In the Garden of Eden, man originally was part of nature; he was near to God. But after he had eaten from the Tree of Knowledge, he was expelled from the Garden. Beginning to "know" and to "think," he lost the immediacy of his creaturely existence.

Plants and animals are organic parts of the cosmos. Nature cares for them and does, as it were, their thinking for them. An animal lives exclusively in the present. At certain times it is completely possessed by an urge; when the urge is satisfied it is completely free of it until a new urge is aroused by biological necessity. Man, however, has eaten from the Tree of Knowledge. Hence he is perpetually torn by two opposing drives. He wants more knowledge, greater power, richer satisfactions for his ego yet can achieve them only at the cost of his growing isolation from nature. At the same time, he feels this growing isolation and desperately seeks to overcome it, to become one with nature once more so that it may enfold and protect him. He is a fleck of dust in the infinity of the cosmos yet conscious of his position; alienated from nature, he desires more than anything else to be part of it.

III

In this tension Gordon discovers the source of *religion*. It is rooted in the fundamental tension of human existence: The tension between man's cosmic isolation, his alienation from the world caused by his intellectual nature, and his deep longing for the healing of this breach and the recovery of cosmic unity. Religion is the profound awareness of the absolute unity of all reality. In the religious thought or act, the soul becomes united with the soul of the world. Through religion man begins to feel once again that he is an inseparable and organic part of creation as if his self were identical with the Self of all being.

God cannot be approached through the intellect; but man can reach God in an immediate living relationship. With the psalmist, Gordon says, "My soul thirsteth for God, the living God," (Psalm 42). A mystery to the intellect, God cannot be known; but He can be experienced and lived.

The unknowability of God's nature is a concept which is firmly rooted in Jewish tradition and had received systematic treatment by Maimonides. If God Himself is unknowable by definition, we can "know" Him only through the inference from effect to cause. The root of the world can be known only by its tree. Gordon never asks whether God is a person; he knows that any attempt to define God in human terms must fail. His starting point is man's age-old question: Does the world possess light, meaning and purpose, or is it dark, purposeless, an accident of evolution? Is the world governed by a blind cosmic force indifferent to human welfare, or is there a divine law which is refracted, be it ever so weakly and imperfectly, in our logic and moral standards? Are our ethical norms merely social conventions, or are they in some way images of a divine reality? These questions trouble Gordon constantly. Can we say that life has meaning in the face of a world that is filled with suffering, torn by hatred, beset by folly, pervaded by pain and cruelty? Why are there so many tears in the world? Why do even animals groan heartrendingly at night? Why is it that of all beings man, knowing more and feeling more deeply than all other beings, is the most rapacious of beasts, inflicting suffering upon others, yet suffering himself universally? In the face of this reality, can we believe the ground of the world to be light rather than blind chance?

Gordon's answer is simple: If life has neither meaning nor purpose, the wisdom and harmony which we actually find in the world become wholly incomprehensible. God's nature is unintelligible to us; His justice cannot be measured by human standards. Nevertheless, we can assume that our sense of justice, however rudimentary, and our efforts at moral conduct, however inadequate and fumbling, are part of a larger cosmic pattern and rooted in the justice and morality of God, a refraction of that light for which our soul longs.

IV

Gordon's friends and associates found it difficult to accept his religious notions. For them religion had become ossified, irrelevant, a thing of the past. Nietzsche and Marx had taught them that God was dead. Gordon attempts to meet their objections by making a distinction between *form* and *content* in religion. He concedes that as far as form is concerned, religion has lost much of its vitality. The content of religion originates in the religious individual; it is the expression and embodiment of his sense of cosmic unity and purpose. Form in religion, however, is a product of the group. A group changes and develops more slowly than an individual does and therefore tends to lag behind. Hence form never catches up with content. Forms are preserved even though the notions or emotions behind them have changed or disappeared. Men tend to sanctify religious forms at the expense of religious content. A religiously sensitive person may, therefore, be compelled to accept outmoded religious forms or to withdraw from the fellowship of his people. Even at the highest level of its religious development, the Jewish people did not escape the oppression of content by form. The prophets had been prepared to advocate the abolition of animal sacrifices. But the people had assigned such a position of centrality and sacredness to the practice after their return from the Babylonian exile that prayers for their re-establishment have been retained in traditional Jewish worship until today.

Gordon feels that the ossification of *religious form* has been accompanied by an ossification of the *concept of religion.* People claim that religion has lost its capacity to change, develop and renew itself, to stimulate the heart and nourish the mind. Religion is glibly dismissed as a lullaby retained from mankind's infancy or as an opiate for the masses. Outmoded and congealed conceptions or religion prevent man from understanding its true nature and function. In contrast to these views, Gordon claims that, though present-day religious *thinking* may be dead, God Himself can never die. He is a hidden mystery, yet we encounter Him in all we experience. No declaration of philosophers or hypotheses of scientists can destroy this reality. Religion will not die so long as men live and think and feel. Its time has not passed — its time has not yet come. True religion is of the future.

What must be done to revitalize religion? Gordon has little faith in discussions, resolutions, organizational activities. The causes of decay are far too complex for such superficial remedies. The flow of divine power — Gordon uses the Kabbalistic term *shefa* (abundance) — continuously rejuvenates him who lives in close contact with nature. Man cut himself off from this source of rejuvenation when he left the soil and moved to the city. Nature no longer is the source of his inner renewal; he has reduced nature to a quantity of corn or grain or vegetables or wood which he buys or sells. Man's relationship to other men, to things and nature, have lost their immediacy and become purely utilitarian: they are means to calculated ends but possess no value in themselves.

Authentic religion cannot live in such an atmosphere. If man is to rediscover religion, the proper balance between the two powers of the human soul — intellect and intuition — must be restored. The task of the intellect is to be the servant of intuition, its *shamash*, not to overpower and repress it. However, the *shamash* has become the *shemesh* — the sun and master of man's life and civilization. The proper balance between master and servant can be restored only by man's return to a direct and immediate relationship to nature. "Our road leads to nature through the medium of physical labor."[3] The return to nature through labor will enable man to rediscover religion and to regain a sense of cosmic unity and holiness. Gordon's religion may therefore be defined as a *religion of labor*.

Gordon was strongly influenced by Tolstoy who has preached a similar return to nature; but unlike Tolstoy Gordon attempted to practice what he preached and became a laborer during the second half of his life. Gordon's views also have an affinity to the European intuitionalism of his time, represented by thinkers who since Nietzsche had warned against the dangers of "intellectualism," the excessive reliance upon the purely analytical forces of the intellect which should be subordinated to intuition, the true power of man's soul.[4] However, Gordon was too deeply steeped in Jewish tradition to underestimate the importance of the intellect for life. His aim was not a one-sided glorification of instinct and animal drives but a genuine synthesis between intellect — the "world of infinite reduction" — and intuition — the "world of infinite unfoldment." His views concerning the need for the establishment of a Hebrew university illustrate his concern. Long before the Hebrew University was founded in 1925, people had debated whether a university was needed by a people that was returning to the soil and to manual labor. Gordon favored its establishment for two reasons. The Jews of the diaspora would be able to give their children an education in Palestine; and he anticipated that a strong and mutually enriching relationship between the university and labor in Palestine could be developed. The graduates of the university would find their way to the soil, and labor to the university. Gordon never saw a conflict between the return to nature and intellectual development. Mankind's task as well as the specific task of the Jew in Palestine were not to descend to intellectual barbarism but to correct the one-sidedness of a purely intellectual approach to life by developing the powers of intuition as well.

V

Gordon was a socialist but, like Martin Buber, opposed to socialism in its Marxist form. He regarded Marxism merely as another creation of the intellect, a product of city and factory, of a technological and capitalistic civilization. The aim of Marxism is the reorganization of the social order, not the renewal of the human spirit. It concentrates on externals to the total neglect of inner factors: It seeks to change man by changing the regime instead of seeking to change the regime by changing man. All attempts to transform human life through the introduction of a new social order are doomed to failure if they do not begin with what must come first: the living human being.

A genuine inner renewal of society can be achieved not by an accidentally and superficially related mass but only by an organically united community, the people. Nature itself has created the people as the connecting link between the cosmos and the individual. To use Gordon's metaphor, the people is like a funnel which receives the infinity of the cosmos in its wide opening and channels it through its narrow opening into the soul of the individual. There is a cosmic element in peoplehood.

According to Gordon, a people is an organic cosmic unit created by nature itself. Mankind represents the unity not of states but of peoples. A state is a political community organized around abstract legal principles. A people is a natural community embodying a living cosmic relationship. (Hermann Cohen, in consonance with his rationalism, had taken the opposite position and placed state and law as the creations of man's reason above the nation as the creation of "mere" nature.)

For this reason cosmopolitanism must be replaced by what Gordon calls cosmo-nationalism. Cosmopolitanism is based on the assumption that the individual can be a citizen of mankind directly without being a member of a specific historic people or national group. This assumption is an illusion. Such an individual and such a mankind are mere abstractions. There is no such thing as a man *per se*. There are only men who are Russians, Germans, Frenchmen. True universalism is based on cosmo-nationalism, the development of a new brotherly relationship between nations, the cooperation of nations, each of them aware of its responsibility towards the cosmos of which it is an organic part.

Gordon uses the terse phrase *am-adam*, "people-humanity," "people-incarnating-humanity," to express his thinking on the role of the people in the fulfillment of man's destiny. Man was created in the image of God. Gordon adds that the people has to be created in the image of God, too. This "people-incarnating-humanity" is the new ideal which Israel, returning to its land, is to exemplify in the eyes of all mankind.

Gordon's cosmo-nationalism has genuine universalistic implications. No people must ever be permitted to place itself above morality. Gordon will have no truck with those forms of nationalism that condone acts by the whole people which are crimes if they are committed by an individual. A people incarnates humanity only to the extent to which it obeys the moral law.

The individual incarnates humanity through his membership in the *am-adam* which is living up to its cosmic and moral obligations. Here Gordon saw the great challenge which the Jew faced in Palestine. The recreation of such a nation — its *realization* — was to be the contribution of the reborn Jewish people to mankind. The creation of a nation which, at the same time, would be an integral part of humanity is an extension of the original work of creation:

> "Without the nation that is part of humanity there can be no humanity; the individual cannot be a human being. Who should know this better than we, the children of Israel? We were the first to proclaim that man is created in the image of God. We must go farther and say: the nation must be created in the image of God. Not because we are better than others, but because we have borne upon our shoulders and suffered all that which calls for this. It is by paying the price of torments, the like of which the world has never known, that we have won the right to be the first in this work of creation. Our torment will generate in us the strength to accomplish this creative task. All kinds of refuse and matters of little worth make up the fuel that produces a bright light. In the same way we have transformed our untold suffering and anguish into a divine light; and we shall make it manifest when we create the nation that is one with humanity, the nation in the image of God."[5]

Did the new Jewish nationalism possess the moral and cosmic qualities which Gordon demanded? He saw the crucial test in the attitude of the Jews towards the Arabs. He never tired of stressing that the land belonged to both peoples and that that nation had the greater claim upon the land which suffered more for its sake. His attitude toward the Arabs was informed by the injunction of the Bible concerning "the stranger that sojourns in thy midst." "Our relations to the Arabs must rest on cosmic foundations. Our attitude toward them must be one of humanity, of moral courage which remains on the highest plane, even if the behavior of the other side is not all that is desired. Indeed their hostility is all the more a reason for our humanity."[6]

When Gordon drafted the statutes for the guidance of labor settlements in 1922, he incorporated the following clause:

> "Wherever settlements are founded, a specific share of the land must be assigned to the Arabs from the outset. The distribution of sites should be equitable so that not only the welfare of the Jewish settlers but equally that of the resident Arabs will be safeguarded. The settlement has the moral obligation to assist the Arabs in any way it can. This is the only proper and fruitful way to establish good-neighborly relations with the Arabs."

Gordon did not consider himself a utopian. He was convinced that his concept of the *am-adam* could be made operative and effective in the field of politics. It would eliminate the desire of groups or nations to increase their power and generate a spirit of universal human solidarity in which each nation would be prepared to give as well as to take. Such giving is radically different from a political compromise in which one group bargains with another and finally makes a concession for tactical rather than moral reasons. In this spirit Gordon called upon his people to make sacrifices for the benefit of the Arabs and other national groups in Palestine without any palpable and immediate advantages beyond the hope of ultimate solidarity with them.

VI

Gordon hoped for a renaissance of the Jewish religion in Palestine. Every religion embodies a cosmic as well as a historic element. During the centuries of exile, the Jewish religion had been severed from any relationship with nature. Only the historical element had remained. The divorce of the Jewish people from nature had stymied the development of the Jewish religion. Gordon hoped that the new life in Eretz Israel would restore the cosmic element to its proper position in Jewish experience. At the same time he cautioned against any attempt to revolt against the historic element and to eliminate from Jewish thought and life the insights and values which had emerged during the centuries of exile and persecution. We must not disregard or renounce the new ideas and values which were contributed to our thinking by the various cultures and environments in which we lived. We can retain the best of the Jewish past only if we do not permit our historical heritage to be swept away and replaced by European culture. In defending the importance of tradition, Gordon became involved in an impassioned controversy with two friends, the poet Yosef Brenner and the poet and writer, Micah Joseph Berdichevski, who opposed the ethical core of Judaism even more than its rites and practices and went so far as to say that Jewish history had followed a wrong course ever since Sinai.

Berdichevski's views were representative of the anti-religious sentiments which characterized the Hebrew literature of his time. Hebrew literature had served as the main weapon in the struggle against the ossified ritualism and orthodoxy of the Polish-Jewish *shtetl* during the second half of the 19th century. The poems of Judah Leib Gordon, the great poet of the first generation of Hebrew writers, are replete with anti-religious sentiment to such a degree that their polemical force often obliterates their significance as poetry. The generation after Judah Leib Gordon heard Berdichevski advocate the complete secularization of Judaism. Strongly influenced by Nietzsche, he called for a "transvaluation" of the traditional Jewish values, a radical reorientation of Jewish sentiments and aspirations as a prerequisite for the rebirth of the Jewish nation. The entire road taken from Sinai had been an aberration. "This is the secret of our exile, our outer as well as our inner exile: that we were content to accept humiliation and not retaliate in kind — humble as a reed." Redemption from the exile requires redemption from the mentality of the exile; the Jew must once again learn to value strength, not books; physical courage, not the endurance of spiritual meekness; the healthy instincts of the natural man, not a pale and bloodless spirituality.

Saul Tschernichovsky echoed the same sentiments in his poem "Before the Statue of Apollo" in which he glorifies the sensual culture of ancient Greece and declares, "I am the first Jew who returns to thee." A curious confusion of values and ideas characterized the thinking of these modern Hellenizers. They exalted the Maccabean struggle against the Hellenizers as the symbol of the great victory of the national idea over foreign influences. Yet at the same time a poet like Tschernichovsky who is representative of the entire movement preaches a return to *Apollo*, thus glorifying the very ideas of a Jason or Menelaus against whom the Maccabees had taken up arms.

However, the secularizing and anti-religious tendency of modern Hebrew literature did not remain unchallenged. The poet Feierberg wrote an open letter to Berdichevski in which he pointed out the danger of his approach. Men like Aḥad Ha-am, Bialik and Gordon spoke out similarly. Gordon's opposition is particularly significant because it came from the ranks of the Jewish labor movement which, like the European socialism of the 19th century by which it had been nourished, was largely blind and often hostile towards religious values. Gordon rejected Berdichevski's position as "assimilation in a Hebrew garment." "What is assimilation," he writes, "what is the wholesale destruction of a people whose very life substance is its spiritual nature, if not the destruction of this very national characteristic? Is the desire to change, to alter our character until it is quite different and new, anything but the desire to destroy our national essence down to its very roots?" "These men wish to preserve the wine while breaking the keg. They certainly do not wish the Jewish people to perish. In fact, they regard their ideology as the means to save the Jewish people from spiritual destruction. In reality, however, their ideology can only lead to disaster."[7]

The controversy between Gordon and Berdichevski touches not merely upon the central theme of modern Hebrew literature but of contemporary Jewish history. It symbolizes the continuing struggle between the forces which strive to make the Jews a nation like all other nations, and those which see in the Jewish people the instrument for the realization of the *idea* of Israel. The future character of Israel the people and of Israel the state will depend on the question whether the spirit of Aaron David Gordon will eventually lose or win in this struggle.

CHAPTER SIX

RAV KOOK: ALL REALITY IS IN GOD

The Balfour Declaration had been issued shortly before the end of the First World War. Britain had pledged her support of the Zionist hope for the establishment of a Jewish national home. An atmosphere of Messianic expectation pervaded Palestine. The redemption of the Jewish people, the fulfillment of Israel's national aspirations and destiny seemed at hand. Towering above the people who had prayed, waited and prepared for the moment of fulfillment was the personality of Abraham Isaac Kook, the Chief Rabbi of Jerusalem.

Kook felt with every fibre of his being that the return of the Jewish people to Israel was far more than a political event or an experiment in colonization; it had a profound religious significance. In his Talmudic academy he had long placed special emphasis on the study of those sections of the Jewish codes which dealt with agriculture and the Temple service, that is, those laws which were valid and applicable only in an autonomous Jewish state and whose study had therefore been neglected for centuries.

The period of Rabbi Kook's leadership as Chief Rabbi of Jerusalem and later as the Ashkenazic Chief

Rabbi of the entire country (1919 to 1935) coincided with one of the great formative stages in the development of the future Jewish state. During that period the Jewish population grew from 90,000 to about 400,000. For centuries Jewish life in Palestine had been dominated by the "old" *yishuv*, the men who had come to die and to be buried in Palestine's holy soil or to sanctify God in His holy city through a life of prayer and study, sustained by the philanthropy of fellow Jews all over the world. They lived in the narrow alleys of the Old City, insulated from contact with the political and social realities of Palestine.

After the turn of the century and especially after the Balfour Declaration, a different kind of immigrant entered the country. Young men arrived in increasing numbers. Many were motivated by the ideals of Jewish nationalism; others, schooled by the Russian revolution or trained by the youth movements of Central European socialism, came to Palestine to realize their ideals of a socialist society in the Zionist communal settlements. They were indifferent to religion and often rejected it completely. The old *yishuv* and the new represented two different worlds. The gap between them seemed unbridgeable.

Rav Kook became the link between the two worlds. He bridged them in his own personality. His learning and strict traditionalism identified him with the old *yishuv*. Born in Grieve, a small town in northern Russia in 1865, he had attended *ḥeder* from earliest childhood and had shown himself to be a student of such exceptional gifts in his Talmud studies that he became known as *illui*, child prodigy, at the age of nine. He continued his studies as the favorite pupil of Rabbi Naftali Zvi Yehuda Berlin, the famous head of the Yeshiva of Volozhin, and he came to Palestine in 1904 in order to become the Rabbi of Jaffa. After the First World War which had caught him in Europe, he returned to Palestine in 1919 in response to a call to become the Chief Rabbi of the Ashkenazic community of Jerusalem. His background and learning as well as his intense piety had earned him the respect of the old *yishuv*.

At the same time, he who had come to Palestine out of a passionate love for Zion, was deeply sensitive to the aspirations of the young pioneers, and he won their affection and respect by his understanding of their Zionist and socialist ideals even though his own convictions and their European "isms" were worlds apart.

I

Rav Kook himself would not have used a phrase such as "worlds apart." He saw no dichotomies in the world. The world possesses a harmony which is indivisible and which it derived from its very origin, its divine source. Indeed, the concept of harmony is one of the central categories of Kook's thought, who in Professor Nathan Rotenstreich's words "bridged all abysses and sees reality and man in an all-embracing view."

At the risk of oversimplification, Kook's system can be defined as a mystical "panentheism." *Pan en theo* — everything is in God. Rav Kook was not a pantheist. Pantheism identifies God and the world and thus tends to eliminate the personal God of tradition. Kook maintains that all reality is *in God*, not that reality and God are identical.[1]

Hermann Cohen had thought that the uniqueness of God could be vouchsafed only by conceiving God as wholly different from the world. Therefore he had made a radical distinction between the "being" of God and the "becoming" of the world and compared their relationship to that between a light and its shadow. Rav Kook denies any degree of reality to a world that is separated from God. There can be no duality; a divine unity permeates the all. Kook does not shy from dithyrambic language in order to describe this divine essence behind the multiplicity of the visible phenomena. "All length, height, depth; every light, rejuvenation, fertility, process; every impulse in poetry and every spark of reason; lights which flame eternally and lights which burn for a moment only; all this sublime reality is in truth nothing but refractions of God's being, sparks of divinity . . . . Genuine science teaches us the unity of the world, of body and soul, of imagination and reason, of the lowly and the exalted . . . . This truth far transcends the limited findings of the scholarly disciplines which man has designed to illumine and clarify his world. We cannot make any absolute distinction between various levels of being; their difference is merely one of degree.

The world unites and reconciles all contradictions; all souls and all spirits, all events and all things, all desires, drives and enthusiasms: everything is part of a larger order and kingdom. God is King."[2]

For Kook, the quest for truth and understanding begins with the attempt to discover this larger order, the deeper unity behind the chaos and multiplicity of surface phenomena which man encounters in the world. The seeker for truth wants to push beyond the fragmentariness of conceptual knowledge and discover the underlying principle, the true essence that gives unity and cohesion to the diverse data and phenomena of the external world.

Kook's theory of knowledge had been decisively influenced by the Hasidic doctrine that the world of the senses is merely a veil and the outer appearance of things merely their "shell," while their real essence is the spark of holiness that dwells in everything. Hence reason is incapable of solving the problem of cognition. Rational reflection and analysis can at best provide us with disconnected scenes of various aspects of life; they cannot give us a picture of the whole of reality nor envisage the dynamic, unifying substance that underlies the whole of experience. Ultimately, man can grasp reality and perceive truth only through the non-rational faculty of his inner vision and the power of his imagination.

II

Kook is literal in his denial of the existence of a world or reality that are separate from God. He develops this thought in a comment on the words of the prayer book, "What are we? What is our life? What our goodness and justice, what our strength and power?" These words are usually taken merely as a description of man's finitude and limitation. For Kook they are the assertion of the literal non-existence, separate from God, of every creature. The prayer book employs so many different terms because human language cannot express fully the absolute and unconditional extent of the nothingness of a human existence that is separated from God. The world would be an illusion, unreal, if it were not grounded in God, the source of all being. But the world is no illusion. By being grounded in God, every thing or event, even the most trivial, mirrors God. "Every spark carries the seed of infinity;" the diversity of seemingly unrelated events and things attains an inner unity.

Kook knows that man cannot live every moment of his life with the complete awareness of the all-pervasive oneness and uniqueness of God and the consciousness that all reality exists only in so far as it is rooted in God. The soul is not always capable of experiencing a union with God. There are times when we are unable to respond to the "Hear, O Israel" with utter sincerity and complete surrender. Therefore, this passage is followed in our prayer books by the sentence, "Blessed be His glorious kingdom for ever and ever." The *shema* affirms God's Oneness; however, the second sentence no longer speaks of God Himself but of His Kingdom. Whenever his soul is separated from God, man turns from within to without, from God to the world. Unable to experience a direct and unmediated inner union with God, man seeks to discover a divine unity in the world through secondary media — the processes of thinking, observing, reasoning; through scholarly assumptions and hypotheses. For this reason the second passage of the *shema* is said silently throughout the entire year except on the Day of Atonement. On that day, all corporeality, finiteness and this-worldliness are transcended; God and the world are one; the Creator and His creatures are united. The Day of Atonement anticipates the full redemption of the world from its separation from God. Therefore, the second verse may be recited aloud and indeed triumphantly on Yom Kippur.

The separation of the world from God was brought about by Adam's sin. Man was caught in what Kook calls the "net of forgetfulness;" he forgot his true origin as a creature and erroneously ascribed autonomy to himself and the world. Man's separation from God can be overcome by *teshuvah*, repentance, man's "repentant return." There are two types of *teshuvah*: *teshuvah* can be general, involving the spiritual elevation and moral improvement of the world; or it may be the "return" of the individual who seeks to improve and elevate his life. The repentant return of every individual affects the whole world; at the same time, every improvement of civilization, of the social and economic order, is part of the repentant return. Hence, *teshuvah* is an act that has moral, religious, social, and cosmic connotations at one and the same time. "The power of *teshuvah* in all worlds makes everything return and reunite with the full reality of divine perfection."

The return of everything to its divine source is the completion of the cosmic evolutionary process. Thus Kook gives a cosmo-religious interpretation and endorsement to Darwin's theory of evolution which, in his judgment, comes closer to the spirit of Jewish mysticism than any other concept developed by modern science. Kook vigorously rejects the religious objections which have often been raised against Darwin's theory because of its seeming incompatibility with the account of creation found in Genesis. He points out that even the ordinary man in the street knows that the creation story cannot be taken literally and that it requires interpretation in symbolic and metaphysical terms to yield its mysteries.[3] Like Darwin, Kook feels that there is a force behind the evolutionary process which pushes it ceaselessly forward. Unlike Darwin, however, who conceives the blind struggle for survival as the force driving all creatures forward, Kook sees the moving force in the yearning of all that exists for the full discovery of God and for the return to Him.

Thus the world of reality is neither a blind mechanism nor a lifeless machine which is gradually running down until it will be arrested in motionlessness. The real world is full of light and life; it is not static but dynamic; it is not standing still but advancing, aspiring, filled with a drive for perfection. This inner current of creativity which fills the world, unlike Bergson's *élan vital*, is not blind, spontaneous, undirected. For Kook, the divine flow has purpose and direction: it derives from God and impels all creation onward and upward toward perfection and the reunion with God as the final goal of human and world history.

Man's yearning for God develops ever new forms. Contradicting Koheleth's claim that there is nothing new under the sun, Kook maintains that "there is nothing old under the sun." Evolution is ascent involving all creation. No entity can isolate itself from this ascent; everything strives toward the one great aim — return to God. The whole of creation is an organic unit; *one life* pulsates in all reality. Dormant in the minerals, already awakened in the plants, fully alive in the animals, it pervades all reality including men, despite their political and racial divisions, and even touches the angels on high. All creatures are fragments of the one world-soul which is the source of all being and orders the world with wisdom. The higher the degree of evolution, the more does the organic character of the world become manifest; and the evolutionary process will have reached its goal when all men will unite their will with the will of God and God's name will be acknowledged and revered in all the world. Kook never tires of describing, in ecstatic and poetic language, mankind's hours of grace and fulfilment when the separation from God will be ended and the whole of creation will be infused with God's light of holiness.

Although the whole of creation is an organic unit, man occupies a special place within the organic unity of all creatures. He stands in the center of the universe. The fact that the earth is only a tiny particle of matter in the vast expanses of the universe which modern astronomy has been unfolding does not detract from man's special position and "the centrality of his soul in relation to all being."[4] For Kook, man is the focus of the expanding, growing, aspiring universe. Man can dominate and shape the natural forces of his environment. Above all, nature lifts itself to ever higher levels through *man*, striving through him and together with him to come ever closer to its divine source.

Man is not left unaided on his road to holiness and sanctification. He is guided by the example and inspiration of some rare individuals, men whom Kook calls "princes of holiness" and "giants of faith" (*adirei ha-emunah*). Their personality embodies the spirit of holiness and therefore they stand in the very center of the cosmic drama of redemption. "There are giants of faith, great souls, whose actual attachment to God — *devekut* — is continuous. These men are the pillars of the world .... Their merit has preserved wisdom for mankind and has transformed it into a living, beneficial force which enhances and enriches mankind until it will ultimately reach perfection."[5]

III

A profound question remains. Is perfection possible? Perfection implies the absence of evil; perfection can be attained only if evil can be eliminated. But how can man believe in the possibility of ultimate perfection, in the face of the stark reality of evil that exists in the world?

Kook answers this question by negating its validity. He uses a new and daring interpretation of the Biblical story of the Tree of Knowledge in the Garden of Eden in order to make his point. Adam's disobedience may have brought about the separation of the world from God; but the notion that evil exists is in itself a consequence of man's separation from God. It reflects a partial view of reality, not a view that looks at the cosmos as an organic whole. *There is no such thing as evil*. If we look at the cosmos as a whole we find that everything is good, for evil is but the good still incomplete, perfection not yet fully realized. Life is a constant process of growth toward perfection, a progression from less perfect to increasingly more perfect states of being. Where complete harmony and unity have been achieved, evil no longer exists; everything is wholly good. Hence evil is not an intrinsic, inevitable aspect of life; it is man's unfinished task in the world. It can be overcome and eliminated in the course of time. The function of this so-called evil is to push evolution ahead until men will realize that the distinction between good and evil is unreal.

Rav Kook puts it daringly: "Just as the righteous praise God, so do the wicked. And just as God's praise ascends from paradise, even so does it ascend from the netherworld, until in the end everything will ascend to be purified [literally: sweetened] and sanctified."[6] The theodicies in which philosophers and theologians attempt to vindicate God's justice and goodness in view of the existence of evil, usually justify their claim that God is good even though evil exists by pointing out that not God but man is responsible for the existence of evil; for man himself, having freedom of choice between doing good and evil, has exercised his choice wrongly and thus brought evil into the world. Kook negates this kind of approach. Evil exists only in man's limited view of reality. For God, there is no evil.

In the same way, death is non-existent. According to the Biblical legend, Adam was punished for his sin of disobedience by becoming mortal. His sin brought death as well as man's fear of death into being. But the return of the world to its source will conquer death. Every improvement of the individual or the world; every act leading toward the achievement of perfection constitutes a step toward the conquest of death by the return of the world to its original state of union with God. Death is a lie; it is an illusion. The very fact that Jewish tradition associates death with ritual uncleanliness is a symbol of its falsehood. What men call death is in reality the intensification or reinvigoration of life.[7] The liberation from the fetters of corporeality is the indispensable means of mankind's self-renewal and the instrument of its progress. Fear of death is the universal disease of mankind, but death is terrifying and inexorable only where man is alienated from the source of his being. If sin brought death into being, *teshuvah*, man's return to the source of his being, will conquer it.[8] The soul is not a mere appendage to the body which perishes together with the body; it is part of that undying current of vitality which returns to its source at death.

Unfortunately, the individual frequently lacks the strength for *teshuvah*, for the struggle against sin and death and for the reunion with God. This struggle requires the collective strength of an entire people. For Kook, this people is the chosen people, God's heritage among the nations — Israel. Israel is not merely a religion with a specific set of doctrines, nor simply a nation with a common past and political future. To him Israel is what its name signifies: a warrior of God, a people which has taken upon itself the task to battle for God and which therefore feels responsible for the fate of the divine in the world. This struggle for God and against death is nothing less than the struggle for a new form of consciousness freed from the illusion that death is a reality. No defeat can discourage him who feels called to share in the struggle. Death is an imperfection of creation and Israel's task is to remove it.

IV

The central role which Kook assigns to Israel in the cosmic drama reflects not only his thinking about the nature and significance of Judaism but also his passionate love of Israel. Like Rabbi Levi Yitzchak of Berdichev who, 150 years earlier, had dared to challenge God and take him to task for his seeming injustice to his people Israel, Kook lovingly affirms the literal truth of the ancient prayer, "Thy people are all righteous." Israel is righteous. It cannot do wrong. It never sins. A Jew may seem or pretend to do wrong, but in his heart he remains pure and unsullied. Since Kook denies in principle that evil exists, he would have been consistent had he also denied that a man can be an evil-doer. However, when Kook speaks of his people, he is guided not solely by logic but by love. He writes in one of his letters, "I am grateful to God that He filled my heart with love for Israel. I was granted this love not on account of any wisdom or righteousness I might possess but on account of His infinite mercy and love."[9]

It was out of this spirit of love for every member of his people that Rav Kook rose in defense of the "godless" *ḥalutzim* who had entered the country after the end of the First World War, despite the opposition and at times bitter hostility of the extreme orthodox element in Jerusalem which his actions aroused. A group of pietists once criticized Kook for defending these young men who "trampled everything underfoot" and were desecrating the sacred soil by their religious indifference and transgressions. Kook responded that in ancient Palestine the Holy of Holies had been the most sacred part of the Temple. Its holiness was so great that only the High Priest was permitted to enter it, and even he could do so only once a year, on Yom Kippur, the most sacred day of the Jewish calendar and only after he had performed a complex ritual of purification. However, when the Temple was being built and the Holy of Holies was being constructed, the artisans and their assistants were permitted to enter with their tools, in their working clothes, and without any preparatory acts of purification. In the same way, Kook argued, we are currently engaged in the process of building the Holy Land. The *ḥalutzim* are the working men of our generation. Leave them alone. They are needed. They are building the Holy of Holies. When the building of the land will be completed and Palestine will have become a Jewish commonwealth, there will be time for the application of the traditional standards of piety.[10] Kook firmly believed in the fundamentally religious character of the Jewish soul. He knew many Jews violated the divine law. However, defection from the Jewish law is a transitory phenomenon, the result of the abnormalities of Jewish existence during the centuries of exile and dispersion. In Palestine, the Jewish people would ultimately regain their national creativity, liberate themselves from the bondage of alien ideologies, and accept once again the discipline of the divine law.

Thus, his defense of the *ḥalutzim* is grounded not only in his love of every member of his people but also in his concept of the essential character of Israel which he seeks to define in his *Commentary to the Prayerbook*. Israel is rooted in holiness. At the time of the exodus from Egypt and later at Mount Sinai, Israel received an endowment of divinity and holiness. Since then, the holiness of Israel's character and the immediacy of its relationship with God have remained constant despite all changes of life and circumstance which have affected Jewish life, and despite the constantly widening time span that separates every new Jewish generation from the generation of the exodus. Israel's faith will be rooted in holiness for all eternity.

Israel's "election" at Sinai is one of Kook's favorite themes to which he returns time and again. In Kook's loving eyes, Israel has a special genius for holiness. Other nations, he writes in his *Commentary to the Prayerbook*, "have developed other talents: intelligence, morality, aesthetic sense. Israel, however, received that gift through which alone the humanity of all nations can become completed, the capacity for discovering the divine light in every aspect of reality." Kook calls attention to the peculiar linguistic form of the benediction which the Jew pronounces over the Torah. In its first part, it says, "Who has given us His Torah," but it ends with the words, "Who gives us the Torah." The juxtaposition of the two tenses has a profound significance for Kook: the revelation was given in the past yet it continues in every present and will go on forever. Israel's unique relationship to the divine originated in the past; but it is a continuing process which constantly renews itself.

In the Diaspora, Jews may have become alienated from the flow of holiness. But Kook was deeply convinced that the return to the holy land would renew and reactivate Israel's holiness. Palestine was designated by God for the flow of his divine grace. Like Yehuda Halevi before him, Kook felt and taught that a Jew could reach the highest level of piety only in Israel where he could absorb the wisdom of the past, the knowledge and certainty that the divine harmony and unity of the world would ultimately be restored and that the separation of the world from its divine source would be overcome.

But Kook also knew that this process would involve suffering and dangers, and he warned his people especially against succumbing to the danger of secular nationalism. "It is proper to nurture national honor and to seek to enhance it; but national honor is not an end in itself. It can only be the by-product of the realization of our most important task: to testify and be witness in the world to the name and glory of God. Man is weak. Preoccupied with the means — the increase of Israel's honor and status — he may easily forget the end — the glorification and sanctification of the God of Israel and the world. He may forget that the all-embracing mission of Israel must reveal itself through the people of Israel, created by Him for His glory."[11]

For this reason, Kook also rejected every form of militant nationalism which might advocate the use of force for the acquisition of Palestine and the establishment of a Jewish commonwealth. "This is not what God wants. Israel will not complete its historic journey in a storm; God is not to be found in the raging tempest; He can be found only in the still small voice. Israel must not raise her voice in anger or aggressiveness to the outside world. Nevertheless, in the words of the prophets, 'The isles will wait for her teaching' " (Isaiah 42.4). Israel has yet to find the key to the right harmonization of nationalism and universalism. The key is still lacking and therefore the door to the Holy of Holies is still closed.[12] To find the key is Israel's great and crucial task.

Kook knows that the return of Israel to the soil will also be accompanied by a glorification of physical strength and an emphasis on the material aspects of life. "Wherever people have long been deprived of the material goods of life, it is inevitable that they will be inclined to seek the material satisfactions of life. Therefore, people will at first be preoccupied with material reforms; spiritual shortcomings will become inevitable. The emphasis on material goods will become so strong that it will appear to many as if it would destroy all spiritual order. But time and historical perspective will show that the concern with the body and with the physical welfare of the people will also have preserved the spiritual values of the people in their purest form."

V

We have already mentioned that Kook ascribes a special genius for holiness to Israel. The concept of holiness is one of the central categories of his thought, and his major work is, significantly, entitled, *Orot Hakodesh*, (The Light of Holiness). Holiness fills the world.

What does it mean to be holy? It means to be rooted in God. It means to surrender one's life to God to the point of desiring only to be a tool in His hands. Holiness flows into the world without end. It enters into any man who is prepared to receive it, and every man has a predisposition towards it. The spirit of Messianism, of the loving return of every individual to God, pulsates in the whole world, and man's task is to guard the holy sparks which light up everywhere to be at last united into one holy flame.

Kook's concept of holiness also leads him to formulate what can be called the principle of a Messianic sociology. Man's corporate life too must be infused with holiness and realize God's purposes. Only that human association is constructive and lasting which is rooted in God. "There are two ways of establishing peace and concord among men. By nature social beings, men may become part of a community for purely utilitarian reasons, recognizing that existence in a community is to their mutual advantage. This kind of concord exists even among a gang of thieves. Based on mere chance, it cannot last, for it has no true center. Even if it should last for a time, dissension, hatred and internal conflicts will destroy it in the end. A true union of individuals and groups must rest on the fact that we are all brethren, children of our Father in Heaven. It must rest on the insight that only in peace and concord can all our potentialities for wisdom, justice and righteousness find realization."[13]

The Messianic kingdom will be a kingdom of *peace*. To discover the light of Messianic peace is the ultimate goal toward which all human effort must be directed. In the discovery of this light man's thoughts and inclinations become united with the totality of the infinite Divine light. Thus Rav Kook's thinking finds its consummation in the vision of perpetual peace, just as Hermann Cohen's *Religion der Vernunft* had ended in a similar vision of enduring peace as the crowning achievement of man's quest for moral perfection.

VI

On the morning of Simḥat Torah, one or two years before his death, I saw Rav Kook passing through the Jaffa Gate on his way to the Wailing Wall. A group of disciples followed him, more dancing than walking, clapping their hands to accentuate the rhythm of the old Hebrew folk song they were singing, "David, King of Israel, he lives and endures forever." Kook, dressed in festive rabbinic garments, walked in front of them. His face was pale, his eyes were nearly closed. He seemed completely oblivious of the singing around him, of the loving admiration of his followers, of the curiosity and interest which he and his pupils aroused. At that moment, he was oblivious of the world. Nothing around him mattered. It was the festival of the Torah and he was wholly absorbed in the joy of the spiritual union with the Torah and its Giver. To him the world no longer existed. He heard only "The voice of the Beloved, behold He cometh."[14]

Chapter Seven

JUDAH LEIB MAGNES: THE CONQUEST OF PESSIMISM BY FAITH

Judah L. Magnes, founder of the Hebrew University in Jerusalem and its first President, was neither a theologian nor a philosopher. He was not a systematic thinker and he did not attempt to develop a systematic interpretation of Judaism. Nevertheless, he is one of the crucial figures in the development of Jewish religious thought and life in our time, especially in Israel.

Rav Kook (1865–1935), A. D. Gordon (1856–1922), and Judah Magnes (1877–1948) lived in Israel at about the same time. However, the religious life and development of each of these men were wholly different. Kook was firmly and harmoniously rooted in the traditional certainties of faith. Gordon was a seeker; unable to accept the values of the past, he grappled with traditional Judaism in search of a renewal of the sources and forms of religious living. Finding the traditional forms largely lifeless and meaningless, he sought to discover and formulate a new cosmic God-awareness which could revitalize them. Though he was critical of the religious certainties of tradition, he interpreted life and Jewish existence not merely in secular, humanistic or historical terms, but in the framework of his cosmic orientation.

In sharp contrast to these men, Magnes' orientation was wholly political and historical. Born in California, he was trained for the rabbinate at the Hebrew Union College in Cincinnati; yet by temperament and vocation, he was an organizer and man of political affairs. As the young rabbi of a leading reform congregation, he had attempted to organize the disunited and heterogeneous masses of New York City and bring them together in a single, all-embracing and united Jewish community. Later he was among the founders of the Hebrew University, and finally he became involved in the difficult and challenging struggle for reconciliation between Jews and Arabs. He fought his battles in the political arena. However, they were motivated by his religious convictions; for Magnes sought God in history. He was a man of unwavering courage, a courage which was rooted in his religious commitment.

I

During the First World War, Magnes had become a pacifist and pledged himself never to take part in war. But his pacifism was unable to survive Hitler's ascent to power. When the persecution of Jews and Christians started in Central Europe, Magnes began to rethink his position. "Satan is abroad. The incarnation of the devil sits on the German throne. It is the principle of evil made flesh. The devil has unleashed his war, and who can sit back and not take sides, with the devil or against him? I shrink from the blasphemy that ours is the side of God, and that we are His chosen. But what I say is: There the devil is for all men to see, his voice for all men to hear, his deeds for all men to abhor, his plans for all men to frustrate. It is the idol in the Temple, the abomination of desolation, and it is ours to bring it down. Perhaps we may be brought down in the effort, for who knows the ways of God's wrath and punishments? But we must make the effort."[1]

The radical pacifist and conscientious objector became an advocate of war against Hitler.

> "This may seem but a slight change to some, just a change in tactics. But it is in fact a very deep change. I might say an agonizing change. It is virtually a change in religion. For pacifism was (can I say, still is?) a fundamental tenet of the religion of these men. But the matter is even more complicated. For, when a man changes his religion, it is usually in order to accept what he thinks is a higher belief. The change of which I speak is of the opposite nature. It is, with one's eyes open, accepting a lower belief, the belief that the taking up of arms, though never righteous, is inevitable, at this juncture, now that the war has been unleashed. This is apostasy from the pacifist faith. One may still hold this faith, but without having the strength to carry it through at this moment in practice. This is something like a tragedy for man. It is contrary to all their public professions hitherto. There is a small volume of mine, called *Wartime Addresses* which will tell anyone interested what

this may mean to me. Men who were threatened with imprisonment, death, torture of their families on account of their pacifism then, are now no longer pacifists in action. They know that war settles nothing, despite the killing of millions. They know, too, that until millions of men in all the nations refuse war service there will continue to be wars. Yet, now that the war is on, they cannot remain impartial."

This passage is taken from an address which Magnes delivered before the student body of the Hebrew University a few weeks after the Second World War had broken out. The "change in religion" of which he speaks meant for Magnes a profound inner crisis. Only a few weeks before the outbreak of the war, he had addressed an open letter to Gandhi in which he asked for counsel.

"I will ask for your guidance. The question gives me no rest. Like you, I do not believe in any war. I have pledged myself never to take part in a war. My pacifism is passing through a pitiless crisis. I ask myself: suppose America, England, France are dragged into a war with the Hitler bestiality, what am I to do and what am I to teach?"

The letter raised numerous additional questions related to the problem of pacifism, to the situation of Jews in Germany, the relations between Jews and Arabs and Zionism generally. Unfortunately, Gandhi's sole response was a brief formal acknowledgment. Magnes did not receive the guidance for which he had asked; he was thrown back upon his own resources. It may have been Gandhi's silence which first brought him to the soul-shattering realization that perhaps there was no answer to his question; that there could be no guidance; that God had "hidden His face."

II

The war took its tragic course. Saved by the victory at El Alamein, the Jews of Palestine, in helpless agony, began to learn of the terrible fate which was overtaking the Jewish communities of Europe. Magnes' addresses before the student body of the University during that period reflect that agony as well as his own inner struggle. His address at the opening convocation of the new academic year in the fall of 1944 is particularly noteworthy; it intimates the depth of his despair.

> "Is it possible that this can happen under God's heaven? I must raise this question, even though I have no adequate answer. It gives millions of men no rest. The world today faces many fateful problems, but none so momentous as this. Is there a living God for whom all this has meaning? Is there design and purpose? Or, is the universe ruled by a blind, unmoral force, by some *deus absconditus*, who created the world and is no longer interested in its fate — withdrawn, asleep, or gloating over the writhing of his creatures upon the earth? I try to evade this question, and cannot. 'And it was in my heart as a burning fire shut up in my bones, and I was weary with forbearing, and I could not.' Yes, the abyss between the Creator and His creatures is immeasurable, terrifying; and it is the very essence

of the religious problem to struggle unceasingly with the question: Is it possible to bridge this chasm, dare flesh and blood set foot upon this bridge? If today the answer be 'yes,' tomorrow doubts creep in. Today, 'He beholds the light and whence it flows,' tomorrow the eye is without seeing and there is cloud and thick darkness and the shadows of death. The struggle renews itself within the soul each day, each night."

Magnes felt himself driven toward a position of extreme pessimism. He rebelled against science which, in Julian Huxley's words, "refuses to ask questions that cannot be answered;" he rebelled against philosophy which is satisfied to discuss the stark reality of evil in our world with an academic detachment that runs "the danger of representing these tortures and these torturers, not as actual and ever-present, but as a kind of abstraction." And by way of contrast, he quoted a legend from Jewish tradition which tells that when the angels beheld the tortures to which the Romans subjected Rabbi Akiba, they cried out in anguish: "Is this the Torah, and is this its reward?" Magnes castigated both science and philosophy for passively accepting the sufferings of the world; but even more bitterly he accused religion itself — the kind of religion which refuses to face the reality of evil in all its starkness and which blunts and smothers man's full realization of the tragedy of life by giving him a false and superficial sense of complacency. "There is a religious approach which you cannot share. It is the attitude of religious quietism which would guarantee your peace and which enjoins quiet acceptance of everything going on about you. Some of the most moving of the Psalms have arisen out of this spirit. But encountering it in these awful days, it is difficult not to protest."

Magnes raises the same question which Job had posed in Biblical times. But for Magnes even Job does not escape censure, for he raised the problem of God's justice only after he himself had been stricken.

"Yet at the time when God's blessings were resting upon him individually, might he not have known that all was not right *with the world* — suffering and sorrow, and cruelty and the torture of the innocent. He did not rise up against his Creator then, or curse his day. Job's rebellion would have had greater significance had it come from a man in health. We ourselves, through chance, have not been cast into these gas-chambers and furnaces. Does the problem on that account not stare us in the face?

"I have said that I do not know what the meaning is of this desert of thick darkness that shuts us in. But by means of this religious approach I find myself facing in the positive direction, and not the reverse. It is as though two men were together standing on a narrow, obscure path. This path is the pessimism common to both. Then the one turns with all his might in the direction of No, and there he remains standing, while the other turns with all his might in the direction of Yes — yes, there is a meaning to all this.

"Thus turned, this man cannot stand still. He has started on a long and weary road. He wants with all his will to be among those who seek the Face and pursue righteousness. But from that man

God hides His Face. An opaque screen holds him asunder from the living God. For all his trying to come nearer and to touch the outer fringe, he cannot. It will not be given him to appear before the presence, to hear the voice, or to understand the meaning of these massacrings, this wanton butchery. Yet, he can do no other than to persist in his quest to the last, to keep on inquiring, struggling, challenging. He will not be granted tranquillity of soul. But if it be given him to renew the forces of his being day by day and constantly to be among the seekers, the rebellious — that is the crown of his life and the height of his desire.

"It is said of Rabbi Isaac Levi of Berdichev that he spoke thus: 'I do not ask, Lord of the world, to reveal to me the secrets of Thy ways — I could not comprehend them. I do not ask to know why I suffer, but only this: Do I suffer for Thy sake?' For us, too, it would be enough to ask, not what is the meaning of this anguish, but that it have a meaning; and that our need of asking be so sincere that it becomes a prayer: 'Teach us only this: does man suffer for Thy sake, O Lord?' "

In the midst of the war Magnes founded a small religious community, called first *M'vakshei Paneicha*, "Those seeking Thy Face," but later renamed more unassumingly, *Ha-Ol*, the Yoke, — meaning, the yoke of the coming Kingdom of God. For Magnes the acceptance of this yoke signified "acceptance of all suffering in love, but not in joy. Acceptance of the yoke even unto the death of martyrdom; public santification of His Name. To be the servant of God."[2]

Magnes' development was a break-through to God from the very depths of despair. It was a break-through to a God who according to Isaiah is the author of evil as well as of good (Isaiah 45.7). Magnes' religious significance lies precisely in this break-through — in his radical conquest of pessimism by faith. Having passed through an inferno of doubt and despair, he rediscovered God as the foundation and fountainhead of Jewish existence and life.

III

Judaism has frequently been accused of preaching an easy optimism. Schopenhauer called it "wicked." At times, a self-satisfied Jewish bourgeoisie, especially in the Europe of the 19th century, has succumbed to the temptation to identify Judaism with an uncritical faith in the possibility of human salvation through cultural enlightenment and progress. The superficiality and inadequacy of this faith was in the center of Rosenzweig's criticism of his parents' generation and of the world of the *Frankfurter Zeitung*. Authentic Judaism knows that progress is neither automatic nor inevitable, that tragedy is part of the human condition, and that every act of faith is invariably a risk. Faith must be rooted in the recognition of the tragic character of life. Magnes lived and suffered this tragic faith. How deeply he suffered could be seen from the change of expression and the deep lines that came over his face in those agonizing years.

Isaiah defined the function and purpose of Israel's existence to be God's witness in the world. For

Magnes Israel is "a laboratory in which the supreme experiment is being carried on." He found reinforcement for his views in a statement by Leonhard Ragaz, a contemporary Christian thinker, who once said that "to believe in God is easy. But to believe that one day this world will be God's world; to believe this in a faith so firm and resolute as to mold one's own life according to it — this requires faithfulness until death." Whether Jews as individuals and as a group can still break through to this faithfulness; whether the Jewish people can still continue to fulfill its purpose to serve as God's witness in the world, is the question which Judah Magnes left for every Jew to answer when he passed away a few months after the birth of the State of Israel, in October, 1948.

NOTES

Chapter One

FAITH AND REASON

[1] Martin Buber, *Two Types of Faith*, New York, 1952.

[2] I Samuel, 3.1–9.

[3] R. M. Prabhu and M. R. Rao, *The Mind of Mahatma Gandhi*, 1945.

[4] *The Guide of the Perplexed*, translated by Friedlander, p. 3.

[5] Isaiah 55.6.

[6] *Kleinere Schriften*, pp. 132–3; N. N. Glatzer, *Franz Rosenzweig*, pp. 209–210.

Chapter Two

HERMANN COHEN: THE RELIGION OF REASON FROM THE SOURCES OF JUDAISM

[1] Republished in the first volume of Cohen's *Jüdische Schriften*.

[2] Cf. *S. Maimon's Philosophy: Epilogue to his Autobiography*, East and West Library, London, 1954.

[3] Quoted by S. Ucko, *Der Gottesbegriff in der Philosophie H. Cohens*, Königsberg, 1927.

[4] Jacob Rosenheim, in the *Israelit*, 1908.

[5] *Jüdische Schriften*, I, p. 333.

[6] Jeremiah 31.29.

[7] Ezekiel 18.21.

[8] *Religion der Vernunft*, p. 244.

[9] Ibid., p. 122.

CHAPTER THREE

FRANZ ROSENZWEIG: BEYOND LIBERALISM AND ORTHODOXY

[1] Fortunately, we possess an extensive volume of Rosenzweig's letters edited and published posthumously by his widow and Ernst Simon (Schocken, 1935), and N. N. Glatzer's biography, *Franz Rosenzweig's Life and Thought*, New York 1953, based largely on his letters.

[2] *Letters*, p. 649.

[3] Glatzer, p. XV.

[4] Glatzer, p. 28.

[5] *Letters*, p. 672; Glatzer, p. 341.

[6] Glatzer, p. 343.

[7] Glatzer, p. XXV.

[8] I. Maybaum, *Synagogue and Society*, London 1944, pp. 154–156.

[9] Glatzer, pp. 292–293.

[10] *Star of Redemption*, p. 383; Glatzer, p. 302.

[11] *Star*, p. 392; Glatzer, pp. 312–313.

[12] Mekhilta 103b.

[13] *Letters*, p. 100.

[14] *Kuzari*, IV, 23.

[15] *Kleinere Schriften*, p. 108; Glatzer, p. 237.

[16] Cf. Hermann Cohen's *Jüdische Schriften*, II, p. 210 ff.

[17] *Kleinere Schriften*, p. 106; Glatzer, pp. 234, 242, 292.

[18] *Kleinere Schriften*, pp. 107–113; Glatzer, pp. 237–238.

[19] Rosenzweig actually uses the term "Reform Judaism."

[20] *Letters*, p. 593 (To Benno Jacob, May 23, 1927).

[21] *Letters*, p. 426.

[22] *Kuzari*, III, 38.

CHAPTER FOUR

MARTIN BUBER: LIFE AS DIALOGUE

[1] *Die Jüdische Bewegung*, p. 37.

[2] *Hasidism and Modern Man*, edited and translated by M. Friedman, New York 1958, pp. 47–69.

[3] Maurice Friedman, *Martin Buber, The Life of Dialogue* (Harper Torchbooks), New York 1960, p. 16.

[4] Martin Buber, *The Origin and Meaning of Hasidism*, edited and translated by M. Friedman, New York 1960.

[5] *I and Thou* (second edition), New York 1958, p. 11.

[6] *Ibid.*, p. 15.

[7] *Ibid.*, p. 101.

[8] *Between Man and Man*, translated by R. G. Smith, London 1947, pp. 22–23.

[9] Victor von Weizsäcker, "Der Arzt und der Kranke," *Die Kreatur* I, 1, 1926.

[10] English title: *Between Man and Man*, see note 8.

[11] *Psychiatry*: Journal for the Study of Interpersonal Processes, vol. XX, No. 2, May, 1957.

[12] *I and Thou*, p. 76.

[13] *Moses* (Harper Torchbooks), New York 1958, p. 51, ff.

[14] *Ibid.*, p. 130.

[15] *Kampf um Israel*, p. 66.

Chaptfr Five

A. D. GORDON: THE RECOVERY OF COSMIC UNITY

[1] Jael Gordon, in *A. D. Gordon: Sikhronot*, edited by M. Kushnir, 1947, p. 85.

[2] Ibid., p. 90.

[3] *Yesssodot l'takanot moshav ovdim.*

[4] Cf. Max Brod, *Diesseits and Jenseits* I, p. 334 ff.

[5] From the opening address of the World Conference of Hapoel Hatzair and Zeire Zion, Prague, 1920.

[6] "Mibachutz," in *Gordon's Collected Works*, 1952, I, p. 478.

[7] "Ha'arakhat atzmenu," ibid. II, p. 221 ff.

Chapter Six

RAV KOOK: ALL REALITY IS IN GOD

[1] For this important distinction see G. G. Scholem, *Major Trends in Jewish Mysticism*, p. 249.

[2] *Orot Hakodesh* I, p. 405–406.

[3] Ibid., I, p. 560.
[4] Ibid., I, p. 447.
[5] Ibid., I, p. 354.
[6] Ibid., I, p. 147.
[7] Ibid., I, p. 392.
[8] Ibid., I, p. 393.
[9] Ha-Hed, Sivan 24, 1913.
[10] Ibid., Elul 1935.
[11] *Commentary to Prayerbook*, p. 315.
[12] Ibid., Commentary to words of Ps. 24, "Who is the King of Glory?"
[13] Ibid., p. 257.
[14] Song of Songs 2.8.

Chapter Seven

JUDAH LEIB MAGNES: THE CONQUEST OF PESSIMISM BY FAITH

[1] *In the Perplexity of the Times*, Jerusalem 1946, p. 21.
[2] Published by S. H. Bergman in *Haaretz*, Oct. 17, 1949.

SUGGESTIONS FOR FURTHER READING

The following books will be helpful for further study. They have been selected both for their intrinsic value and ready availability to the English reader.

The number of general references in English is very limited. They include Jacob Agus, *Modern Philosophies of Judaism*, New York 1941, (a study of Hermann Cohen, Franz Rosenzweig, Martin Buber, and Mordecai Kaplan), and *A History of Jewish Literature*, by Meyer Waxman, vol. IV, New York 1941. The Hebrew-speaking reader will want to turn to two additional general works, *Haphilosophiah shel Hayahadut*, by Yitzhak J. Guttmann, Jerusalem 1953, and Nathan Rotenstreich's *Hamachshava Hayehudit Ba'et Hachadashah*, Tel Aviv 1951.

Hermann Cohen's works are not yet available in English. Jacob Agus, *op. cit.*, pp. 57–128, contains a systematic study of Cohen's thought and a bibliography of all important works by and on Cohen. In *Religion of Reason*, New York 1936, Trude Weiss-Rosmarin summarizes the main elements of Cohen's religious and philosophical thought, and Steven S. Schwarzschild analyzes "The Democratic Socialism of Hermann Cohen" in *H.U.C. Annual*, 1956.

Franz Rosenzweig's major works are not yet available in English either. However, Nahum N. Glatzer's *Franz Rosenzweig; His Life and Thought*, New York 1953, is an indispensable introduction to the life and work of the thinker. It also contains a complete bibliography of all writings by and on Rosenzweig. Another introduction is *Franz Rosenzweig* by Steven S. Schwarzschild, London 1960, (a publication of the Education Committee of the Hillel Foundation, London).

Most of Martin Buber's writings have been translated into English and are easily accessible. Maurice S. Friedman, *Martin Buber: The Life of Dialogue* (Harper Torchbooks), New York 1960, presents a comprehensive study of Buber's development and thought and contains a complete bibliography of Buber's writings as well as books, studies, and articles about him or various aspects of his thought. Other helpful studies of Buber include Arthur A. Cohen, *Martin Buber*, New York 1957; Malcolm M. Diamond, *Martin Buber, Jewish Existentialist*, New York 1960; and *The Writings of Martin Buber*, selected, edited and introduced by Will Herberg (Meridian Books), New York 1956.

Of A. D. Gordon's writings, only some *Selected Essays*, translated by Frances Burnes, with a biographical sketch by E. Silberschlag, New York 1937 (League for Labor Palestine), are available to the English reader. The life, time, and thought of Rav Kook (none of his major works has as yet been translated into English) are presented by Jacob Agus, *Banner of Jerusalem*, New York 1946, and in a briefer study by Isidore Epstein, *Abraham J. Kook, His Life and Works*, London 1951. A list of "The Writings of Rav Abraham Isaac Kook," by Leonard B. Gewirtz, can be found in *Jewish Book Annual*, New York 1960.

In the Perplexity of the Times is a collection of Judah L. Magnes' major addresses and writings. His life and thought are presented in Norman Bentwich's study, *For Zion's Sake: A Biography of Judah L. Magnes*, Philadelphia 1954.